the VIBE

the ViBE

The marketing handbook for every product, service and industry

Gary Bertwistle

Wrightbooks

First published 2010 by Wrightbooks
an imprint of John Wiley & Sons Australia, Ltd
42 McDougall Street, Milton Qld 4064

Office also in Melbourne

Typeset in Berkeley LT 12/15.4pt

© Gary Bertwistle 2010

The moral rights of the author have been asserted

National Library of Australia Cataloguing-in-Publication entry:

Author:	Bertwistle, Gary.
Title:	The vibe: The marketing handbook for every product, service and industry / Gary Bertwistle.
ISBN:	9781742169736 (pbk.)
Subjects:	Branding (Marketing) Advertising—Brand name products. Trademarks.
Dewey Number:	658.827

Excerpts from *The Castle* reproduced with the permission of Working Dog Pty Ltd. This book is the sole work of the author and publisher.

Extract from Nudie's website on p. 62 reproduced with permission of Nudie Foods Pty Ltd.

Figure 2.1 on p. 41 reproduced with permission of Allen & Unwin.

Cover design by Xou Creative

Printed in China by Printplus Limited

10 9 8 7 6 5 4 3 2 1

Contents

Also by Gary Bertwistle

What Made You Think of That?
Thinking Differently in Business

Who Stole My Mojo?
How to Get it Back and Live,
Work and Play Better

The Keys to Creativity:
How to Unlock Your Imagination and
Creative Potential

Dedicated to the creators of tomorrow's next great ideas.
I hope this book helps to unlock one or two!

About the author

Gary is like a shot of adrenalin to the right side of your brain.
Dan Meiklejohn, General Manager, DB Retail
DB Breweries

Gary Bertwistle is one of Australia's leaders in thinking. He is a keynote speaker whose topics include the thinking behind creativity, innovation, marketing, brand and performance. In 2002 he opened Australia's first creative thinking venue at the Entertainment Quarter in Sydney, called the Ideas Vault, which is used by some of the country's biggest corporations for creative thinking, meetings, seminars and training sessions. He is also the author of three books: *The Keys to Creativity*, *Who Stole My Mojo?* and *What Made You Think of That?*

Gary is the co-founder of one of Australia's leading cycling foundations, the Tour de Cure, which raises money in an effort to cure cancer. The Tour de Cure has raised millions of dollars since its inception in 2007. Gary also founded the Day of Inspiration, a corporate fundraising annual event, which gathers together keynote speakers, entertainers and performers at the Four Seasons Hotel in Sydney for a one-day event in front of a corporate crowd to raise awareness of and funds towards curing cancer.

Winner of the TEC Speaker of the Year Award in 2007 and 2008, Gary is renowned for his simple and easy-going style, passion and drive in helping people to think differently about their life, family, business and Mojo. Visit Gary at <www.garybertwistle.com>.

Acknowledgements

Chapeau

David Lo
Andrew 'Max' Walker
The team at TEC Australia
Austereo — all who have been and gone
The Greek Fisherman
Seth and Muzza

Special thanks

Carolyn Crowther — Three Sixty Agency
Gabbi and Emanda — my brains trust
Katherine, Kate, Hannah, Brooke —
the Wiley team: you have been a delight

Introduction

Over the last few years I've been fortunate to work with hundreds of organisations, both in Australia and overseas, on their marketing and branding. From sole traders right through to multinational corporations, I have been truly staggered by the lack of understanding of how marketing really works. As a result, I felt there was an urgent need for a simple and straightforward book on the topic. In addition, much of the literature that is available to marketers on marketing and branding draws largely on American or European examples and doesn't explore day-to-day examples or case studies of Australian brands and their successes and/or failures, so I have tried to rectify that situation here.

As to the title of the book, I believe that the film *The Castle* is one of the greatest Australian films ever made. There is a courtroom scene that particularly resonates with me, and which illustrates beautifully my perception of marketing and branding. Here is an exchange from that scene between a judge and the solicitor Dennis Denuto:

Judge: What section of the constitution has been breached?

Denuto: What section? There is no one section, it's just the vibe of the thing.

Judge: I'm afraid, Mr Denuto, you'll have to be more specific.

Denuto: Ah, yeah, sure. I was just starting general and then I was getting more specific with it. Just one moment please ... um, I've got it here, it's the Section 51. Ah, second from the bottom.

Judge: The Parliament shall have power to make laws with respect to copyright, patents of inventions and designs of trademarks.

Denuto: It's all part of it, this is what I'm getting at, that's my point. It's the vibe of it.

Judge: Alright, taken. Do you have a precedent which supports this ... 'vibe'?

Denuto: Yes, yes I do ... it's the constitution, it's Mabo, it's justice, it's law, it's the vibe and ... no, that's it, it's the vibe.

And that is just it—it's the vibe. Marketing, branding, communication or whatever term you choose to give it, *is* the vibe. It's all those things and more wrapped into one. For me, nothing sums it up better than Dennis Denuto's words: 'No, that's it, it's the vibe'.

The aim of this book is to give your brand, company, service or product a vibe—a positive vibe that talks *with* people rather than *at* them. Your brand can have a poor vibe, no vibe, a good vibe or an outstanding vibe—it's all up to you. This book will give you plenty of thought-provoking examples of what some of the best brands in Australia and overseas have done to build their vibe. Although I'll be exploring case studies that feature larger corporations, don't think that you need to be an organisation with a large media budget to be able to create the right vibe. I'll also be showing you how smaller organisations or individuals are doing it with little or no money at all. No matter what business, category or industry you're in, the principles and tips in this book are relevant to all.

I have also intentionally set out to write a book that is easy to read and simple to understand, one that breaks through the jargon and helps you to identify the right thinking for your brand. Too many people over-complicate the areas of promotions, marketing and branding to make themselves sound more knowledgeable (and to charge more for their services). Once the thinking behind it is understood, it really is a relatively simple process. There is a great deal of power in having the right thinking behind your brand, especially when you are spending a great deal of money on promotions and marketing—and more often that not, wasting it without realising it. At the end of each chapter is a type of checklist, which is a series of questions to ask yourself to establish whether your brand is on the road to generating a vibe. You should return to these lists periodically to check on the status of your vibe.

The Vibe is about helping you to understand the marketing process and develop the thinking necessary to enable you to create the right look, feel, message and vibe for your brand. Ultimately, it is about putting you and your business on the right track to using your time, energy and money in a more productive and successful way.

Chapter 1

Start at the beginning

When I speak to audiences and ask them about the types of marketing they are undertaking for their brand, product or service, I generally receive the same responses. They're advertising in the press, in trade magazines, on television, on radio, through their website, creating brochures and flyers, providing giveaways and entertainment, engaging in strategic alliances, sponsorship and letterbox drops, using signage, having recognisable uniforms, having business cards, attending trade shows and expos, and so the list goes on. It's all fairly predictable and in my experience doesn't seem to vary greatly across business type, category or even country. It's also *not* marketing.

So the question is, what *is* marketing?

When I pose this question to audiences I usually get answers along the following lines: it's about building awareness; it's creating a need between your customer and the product or service that you manufacture; it's selling your goods for a profit; it's finding out what your customer wants and filling that need; it's having the right product in the right place to fill a customer demand; it's making money.

Although these things are part of marketing and branding, there is one small but crucial element to the discussion that is missing. The question we should all be asking is, *why* should someone buy *your* brand and not someone else's? The answer lies in the marketing. It's what gives the customer a compelling reason to choose your company, service or product over someone else's. You can meet the customer's needs, have people know your product or service, even have people like you, but if the customer doesn't believe there's a compelling reason to choose you, then your marketing isn't working. A good example of this in Australia is Pepsi. Everybody knows it, everybody knows where they can get it, and in fact in blind taste-tests done in Australia for the Pepsi taste challenge many years ago it was shown that most Australians actually preferred the taste of Pepsi to Coca-Cola. Yet in Australia a much larger percentage of people actually drink Coca-Cola. Why is that? Because

Coca-Cola still carries the perception of being 'the real thing'. Coca-Cola has a vibe.

Perception is the key fundamental that every organisation, no matter what size, what it produces or what it provides, must understand. What perception should your customer have of you that will make them choose you instead of someone else? The most difficult, yet also the most important, point for any business or company owner to understand is that perception *is* reality. You can be the most efficient business, have the best range or best customer service, but if your customers don't *perceive* these things about you, then ultimately it won't matter. Too many companies spend their

The most difficult... point for any business or company owner to understand is that perception is reality.

time telling me (the consumer) what they do rather than why they're special. They spend their time convincing me of their history and their range of products without telling me what makes them 'famous' (that is, the most recognised in their category), and why I should buy their product or service. They should instead be focusing on creating a perception in my mind of why they are different from or better than their competitors. If you take nothing else from this chapter except this point, then I believe this book was worth your purchase!

Marketing is the perception that you create in the mind of your customers or clients that gives them a reason to choose you. You can carry a good perception, no perception or a poor perception, but it is this perception that creates the vibe. Once you understand this you can then spend your valuable time learning how to create a strong positive perception that in turn gives your brand a great vibe (which is what we shall do in the coming chapters).

Where does branding come from?

The word 'brand' in a marketing sense dates back to when cattlemen used branding irons to burn identification marks onto their stock so that everyone knew who they belonged to. This is a vitally important concept for you to consider. All of the promotion you do should burn (position) the perception (vibe) you want to own into the minds of your customers or clients. Think about all your marketing material from the last six to 12 months. Have you actually been burning a perception of what makes you different or better into the minds of a clear target audience, or have you simply been doing a great deal of promotion about what you do rather than why you're 'famous'?

I once did some brand work with a very successful mid-sized accounting firm in Brisbane. During my time there, the team came to the conclusion that the firm didn't own any specific perception. Consequently we spent some time deciding what word they wanted to own before they went any further with their brand development. A few weeks later the firm's CEO sent me an email with a link to an article in *The Australian Financial Review*. The article was titled 'Mid-tier firms stay middle of the road' and it was questioning what the mid-tier accounting firms had in common. The author concluded that the answer was 'everything', and therein lay their problem. It seemed that the Brisbane accounting firm I was working with wasn't the only one struggling with the way it was perceived.

In fact I would go so far as to say that this seems to be the problem, not just in accounting, but in most categories. What do most engineering companies have in common? What do most landscape companies have in common? What do most bed linen manufacturers have in common? What do most soaps have in common? And so it goes. Within your category, if you have everything in common with everyone else, then there exists a massive opportunity for you and your brand. The marketing part of brand building is simply the thinking behind the perception. The creation of a brand comes about as a result of all the work done in marketing a particular perception to a target audience. When you have executed it well and have burnt the perception into the mind of your target, that's when you actually become a brand.

The model

Marketing is a battle for the mind of the consumer and as we have seen, it is a battle of perceptions. So, how do you go about creating a desired perception with a customer or client? Following is the marketing model that I use with brands, regardless of their size or industry type:

➤ *Target*. Who are you aiming at?

➤ *Product*. What do you do?

➤ *Position*. What do you want people to think of you?

➤ *Promotion*. How will you tell people about you?

I'll explore each of these elements in turn. I've also included a marketing model checklist on page 14 that you can refer back to, to make sure you're on the right track to creating a particular perception about your brand.

Target: who are you aiming at?

The first question you need to answer well before you start spending any time or money on marketing is: 'Who are you marketing to?' Who would be the perfect client or customer for you and your brand? Your target should be a group of people who share a common issue. They are the core group of people whose issue you believe you can solve better or more cheaply than anyone else, and they will remain your target until someone else comes along who can do it cheaper or better than you.

I'm surprised how often I meet CEOs or management teams who believe they don't need to spend time defining their target, as they feel it is already well understood within their organisation. Generally, I suggest that it is put up for discussion anyway, and nine times out of 10 a considerable amount of time is subsequently spent by the group arguing about who their target actually is. If you don't know who your target is, how is your customer or client supposed to know that you are the one to provide them with the product or service they need?

You must be able to articulate clearly who the perfect user for your company, product or service is. Sometimes this can be done via age groups. For example, a radio station might target 18- to 35-year-old males who love rock music. A target can be anything from 'parents with children aged between nought and five years old', to 'small to medium-sized retailers who sell bed linen'.

Some more sophisticated marketers are also targeting a needs state, which is a mental approach to a problem rather than a specific age, gender, income level, company size or use. Regardless of your industry or category, you need to be very clear as to exactly who you're trying to attract to your product or service. It can take some time for a business to articulate what its target is, but don't be too focused on or worried about how long it takes, because defining your target is a critical first step that must be undertaken before you even start to think about investing in any marketing.

... be very clear as to exactly who you're trying to attract to your product or service.

For example, think about what brand of potatoes you buy. If you're like most people, you'll say you buy brushed, white or pink potatoes. That's because supermarket shoppers don't tend to seek out a specific brand of potatoes to purchase. They're usually looking to purchase big, small, white, pink or brushed potatoes, or even just grab a bag of potatoes, regardless of where they are grown or who produces them. Having worked with some of the biggest potato growers in Australia I can tell you that their target is not the consumer, it is the buyer at Woolworths or Coles. The grower's aim is to get the large supermarket product buyer to purchase its particular brand of potatoes and put them on the shelf. So the primary target for a potato grower is the supermarket buyer, which profoundly affects its marketing strategy.

If, on the other hand, you are looking to buy items such as shampoo, a drink, a razor blade, milk or a dishcloth, then you and I as the end users are the target. When we go to the supermarket we are influenced by our perception of particular brands, and as a result we generally select products based on these perceptions. Our choice of brand is based on the packaging, pricing or marketing that has been undertaken for these products. Consequently, all of these brands must market to you and me. Likewise, if we're buying a drink or a tin of dog food, then the owner of the brand (the marketing manager or CEO) is looking to create a vibe in our mind to ensure we choose their brand over another. In fact, many companies would like to think that the vibe around their brand is so strong that if we walked into a supermarket and couldn't find their product, then we'd go elsewhere to find it. This is known as 'brand utopia'.

So, no matter who your target is, the same vibe must be created in the mind of that target. The potato grower needs to market only to the supermarket buyer; however, the manufacturer of a range of vitamins or coffee needs to market to both the end user and the buyer so that both share a common vibe. It's worth noting that although you may have a couple of different targets for your brand, you must identify who the primary or most important end user is and market to them.

Product: what do you do?

When you have decided on your target, the next question to ask yourself is, 'What is my product?' or 'What is it that my company does?' For most people this is a fairly straightforward question to answer.

Whether you sell real estate, manufacture widgets or provide accounting services, it is likely that you have competitors. In fact, your competitors may well be targeting the same people with exactly the same product as yours, in which case the next question is, 'What is your position?'

Position: what do you want people to think of you?

Your position or positioning statement is the sentence that often sits with a company's logo articulating the personality and/or the advantages of your product. It's the statement that succinctly explains to your target why they should use your product or service instead of someone else's. It should be a short phrase, no more than five or six words long, that communicates why you are different. Your position builds the perception you want to own in the mind of your client or customer. If you don't have a position in your target's mind, chances are you don't own the perception and you could well be a boat floating aimlessly around without a rudder. If you are in this situation, you certainly don't have a well-articulated vibe. As the late British advertising legend David Ogilvy noted, 'People don't buy soap to clean themselves. Most buy the promise that it makes them beautiful. They buy toothpaste to create white teeth, not just to clean their teeth. We're told that oranges are not just for nutrition but for vitality. People buy cars for prestige not travel'.

I'm staggered by how many well-known multinational brands don't have a position. Maybe they've been success-

Positioning is at the core of all marketing and all brands.

ful despite themselves or perhaps through a lack of competition they've been able to build quite a substantial revenue base, but just because you have a business, doesn't mean you have a position. If you don't have a clear position in the marketplace, then you're leaving the door wide open for one of your competitors to outmanoeuvre you. As former world boxing champion Mike Tyson said, 'Everybody has a plan until they get hit'.

In good times and bad it's imperative to have a position in the mind of your target audience. If you've been successful to date with no positioning statement, then consider yourself lucky. Positioning is at the core of all marketing and all brands. The best brands own a perception in the consumer's mind that makes them choose one brand over another. For example, if you were going to buy a pair of shoes, you would automatically have a list of two or three brands that you want to check out. The strongest brands own a perception that puts them at the top of your shopping list. Brands generate this perception by having a vibe. If a brand doesn't have a vibe, it doesn't make your shopping list. Here are some examples of great positioning statements:

- BMW: 'The ultimate driving machine'

- King Gee: 'Any tougher and they'd rust'

- David Jones: 'There's no other store'

- Qantas: 'The spirit of Australia'

- Queensland: 'Beautiful one day, perfect the next'

- John West: 'The best'

- AVIS: 'We try harder'

- Aussie: 'At Aussie, we'll save you'

- Miele: 'Anything else is a compromise'

- Woolworths: 'The fresh food people'

- Samboy: 'The flavour really hits you'

- Hungry Jack's: 'The burgers are better at Hungry Jack's'

- L'Oreal: 'Because you're worth it'.

Once you've established what your position is and have a positioning statement, you're ready to move on to the final part of the marketing model.

Promotion: how will you tell people about you?

Promotion is the part of the marketing model that most companies confuse as being the marketing. Promotion includes all of the activities undertaken to promote and create the perception of what you want your target audience to think about you and why you are 'famous'. It can include television and radio advertisements, brochures, your website, email signatures, podcasts, blogs and so on. It's all the media that help to create the perception of your brand in your target's mind.

Henry Ford, founder of the Ford Motor Company, once said that 50 per cent of the advertising dollar is wasted. The question is, which 50 per cent? If you don't know who you're talking to—that is, who your target audience is—and you don't know what perception you want to own in your target's mind to distinguish you from your competitors, then 100 per cent of your advertising budget is gone right there. The promotion is purely the vehicle that cements the perception. A company, business or individual can undertake all the promotion it likes, but if it's not promoting it's position, then it's wasting time, energy and money.

Generally, this confusion as to what marketing actually is stems from the fact that even in large companies the marketing team is often full of sales-based staff who don't know a great deal about marketing. More often than not there's no perception, there's no ownership of a word, they're just selling as much as they can in order to fuel the bottom line. I constantly meet sales and marketing managers looking after big corporate brands who aren't trained marketers, and without this training there can't be any depth of understanding of the marketing model and its components. What they think is a brand is simply a logo that they put on documents in order to get a sale.

Ninety per cent of businesses that I see today don't actually have marketing managers, they have promotions managers, and there is a big difference. If all your marketing manager or director is doing is putting together nice websites, company profiles, sponsorships, signage and so on without any true perception or positioning statement, then you don't have a marketing manager, you have a promotions manager. The title of marketing or brand manager exists when that person actively takes a perception to your target audience and burns it consistently into their minds. Marketing managers add value to the balance sheet and make you money because of the loyalty that your brand creates, whereas promotions managers will cost you money.

... it's essential to get a real understanding of what marketing and branding is all about...

There are loads of great companies around, but very few great brands. For most successful companies the existence or absence of a strong brand doesn't cause too much concern — that is, until they come up against a competitor who knows their stuff, or what's worse, a strategist who knows how to go into battle and outmanoeuvre you. Even if you've done well until now, it's essential to get a real understanding of what marketing and branding is all about if you are serious about creating a truly great brand that will stand the test of time.

I hope that by reviewing your current marketing materials and gaining more insight into the fundamentals of the marketing model you have by now come to some conclusions about where you and your brand currently stand, and in what areas you need to improve. In the rest of the chapter I'll give you some guidelines to follow that will begin to help you articulate your message and start to give your brand a real vibe.

Checklist: the marketing model

Target
- ☐ Do you know who uses your product or service?
- ☐ Do you know who you should aim your message at?

Product
- ☐ Have you established what the actual product or service you are selling is?

Position
- ☐ Do you have a position?
- ☐ If yes, does it make sense?
- ☐ Is it easy to understand?
- ☐ Does it work with your target?
- ☐ Do you promote your position repeatedly?
- ☐ Does your advertising back up your position?
- ☐ If you do not have a position, do you know what you want to own?
- ☐ Do you know what has to be done to own it?

Promotion
- ☐ Do you know how you will tell your target audience about the perception you want to own?
- ☐ Do you have a promotions manager or a marketing manager?

Random acts of marketing

I've found that many businesses suffer from random acts of marketing (RAM), which are generally undertaken to try to generate sales for the next quarter. RAM may consist of a brochure for a new product launch or a flyer about an end-of-year clearance, a trade expo to sell a new range or taking clients on a golf day to promote your business. They could also be seasonal specials, sales team incentives or even new company profiles. Whatever form they take, RAM end up as a mishmash of marketing bits and pieces that were done for a particular reason at a particular time, but together don't form a cohesive story or create an overwhelming perception of the brand.

Are you guilty of undertaking RAM? I challenge you to do your own audit and lay out your recent marketing materials to see if there's a consistent story that runs through them. While you're at it, see if you even have a positioning statement. Does it appear on any of your documentation?

It's only when you have a consistent story that is delivered well over a period of two, three or even five years that you have the makings of a certain vibe for your brand. As Dennis Denuto says, 'There's no one section, it's just the vibe of the thing'. The sum total of the 'sections' is what will give you the vibe. If you do suffer from RAM, then it's about time you took a step back and spent some time reviewing your marketing model to get back on track.

Own a word

The easiest way to create a strong perception in the mind of your target audience is by deciding on a word that you want to own (make sure it's not already being used by another brand in your category), and then burning it into the mind of your client or customer as a brand. Consider the following examples:

- ⫸ Which toothpaste would you buy to help fight *cavities*?

- ⫸ Which toothpaste would you buy for a great *smile*?

- ⫸ Which is the *safest* car on the road?

- ⫸ Which jeans would you buy if you wanted the *original* jeans?

- ⫸ Which tuna would you buy if you wanted the *best*?

- ⫸ Which car would you buy if you wanted a *hybrid*?

(Answers: Colgate, Macleans, Volvo, Levi's, John West, Toyota Prius.)

Whenever I conduct this exercise with any group, anywhere in Australia, inevitably I get the same answers, because these brands have burnt their 'one' word into people's minds very successfully. That one word might be cavities, smile, safe, original, best, trust, care, love, range, size, leader, experts or specialist, but if you own that word, then half your job is done. If you truly want to build a position that creates a perception in the mind of your target, pick out the word you want to own, and then build a statement (your positioning statement) around it to deliver it as part of your logo.

Successful positioning statements that are built around the ownership of a single word are those mentioned earlier such as 'The fresh food people', 'The burgers are better at Hungry Jacks' and 'There's no other store like David Jones', which have been around for years. These *Owning a single word gives you focus.* companies have spent 20, 30, even 40 years burning their positioning into people's minds. Interestingly, if Woolworths is 'the fresh food people', what does that make Coles? Normally when I ask this question people look at me, laugh and suggest perhaps the stale food people! Can you name Coles's positioning statement?

If your business already has a positioning statement, step back and ask yourself whether it creates a perception in your mind. Some businesses have nice-sounding positioning statements, but when it comes down to it they don't really own a particular word, they're just using a selection of words linked together that sound good. To have an effective positioning statement, you must be able to clearly articulate what you own, and then build a phrase to communicate it.

Owning a single word gives you focus. In the book *Beyond Buzz*, author Lois Kelly put it this way: 'What we need here is an arrow not a flying barn'. Essentially you have two choices when picking out the word you want to own. Either you go for an attribute or you go for an emotion. Attributes are specific measurables such as size, technical specifications, taste, performance or technology. If you can't clearly articulate one of these and deliver on that promise to separate you from your competitors, then go down the route of an emotion — love, care, trust, confidence and so on. Omo washing powder has done this remarkably well through its emotive 'Dirt is good' campaign. The brand turned on its head the idea that when children got dirty it was a problem by formulating the belief that when children get dirty they're actually expressing their creativity. Omo has successfully taken the emotive part of the brand and brought it to life.

I saw another wonderful campaign recently for New Zealand Post. The television commercial begins by showing a young child writing a letter to her dad as part of a school project. Her dad opens the letter while sitting in a board meeting and it reads, 'I hope you're having fun'. Looking around, he realises he isn't having fun, and leaves the meeting to collect his daughter from school. The final shot shows them walking together, eating ice-cream and laughing. It is a beautiful ad that communicates the emotions associated with letter writing and the joy of receiving a letter.

When you own a word or own a category, you outman-oeuvre everyone else. As mentioned earlier, this is the case with Coca-Cola, which is far and away the leader in the cola market. I haven't spoken to any audience in the last couple of years that has known Coke's current positioning statement, yet if you look hard, periodically you'll see it in its marketing. In fact, if I ask an audience for Coke's positioning statement they generally still come back with, 'It's the real thing'. It must be 25 to 30 years since Coke has used that particular positioning, yet it still owns 'the real thing', and still owns the word *real*. If Coca-Cola is the real thing, what does that make all the other colas?

Have you guessed Coke's most recent positioning statement? At the time of writing, it's 'The Coke side of life'.

Create your own category

Imagine introducing yourself to a stranger in an elevator. After exchanging pleasantries, often the next question is, 'What do you do?' followed by, 'Who do you work for?' I'm astonished by the number of senior executives who would not be able to succinctly articulate what their company does in a short elevator ride. This problem as it relates to marketing is that today you don't have the luxury of time to be able to build on your explanation. If this sounds familiar, and you can't or don't own a word, why not take the opportunity to create your own category? One of the key rules of marketing or brand strategy is to own a category.

What exactly do I mean by this? I mean that if you can create a category that meets the imagination of your target audience, then pretty much from day one you will not only become the market leader in that category, you will also own the perception of being the leader. Say you work for a beverage company and you believe there is a need for a new beer. You would be silly to try to come up with a beer that would go head to head with market leaders in Australia such as Victoria Bitter, Crown Lager, Hahn Light or XXXX Gold. Instead you would be better off creating a new category, the same way Foster's did with Pure Blonde, establishing a low-carbohydrate category in the beer market. If you were in a pub and a mate said, 'Grab me a low-carb beer', I'm pretty sure you'd order him a Pure Blonde without thinking about it.

...a small organisation can create its own category and hold its own...

The number one selling mid-strength beer in Australia is XXXX Gold, and it essentially created the mid-strength beer category. The number one premium beer in Australia is Crown Lager and it created that category. The number one imported beer in Australia is still Heineken and the number one Mexican beer in Australia is still Corona. Indeed, the fastest growing beers in the beer category are the ones that created their own category, as these brands have done.

Let's take a look at some other examples of companies that have created their own category. Ashley Munro is an accounting firm in Brisbane that has cleverly created its own category in business accounting. The firm's positioning is 'Guiding entrepreneurial success', a category it created and which it now leads. Similarly, there's a law firm in Queensland that specialises in tough cases. Its positioning is 'Tough case—we're tougher'. As a result of this positioning, the firm has competitors sending work its way and law graduates want to work for the firm because of its reputation for taking on the tough cases.

I have worked closely with a company in Western Australia called Aurenda. It had struggled for many years to work out what its 'elevator speech' was. We spent some time on it one morning and the team was finally able to identify specifically what their category was and how they would articulate it in their elevator speech (between the fourth and eighth floors). It was incredibly rewarding to see how delighted they were and the change in their body language when they finally found a way to articulate what they did. Aurenda is Australia's leading injury cost reduction company, and having articulated that the company went on to become the market leader in this area. In Western Australia Aurenda is receiving a great deal of publicity and media interest from people looking for someone to speak on this topic. This company is a wonderful example of how a small organisation can create its own category and hold its own, even when up against the corporate giants.

There is also a very successful, yet relatively new, brand of car wash in Sydney called Star Café Wash. Since early 2007 the company has gone from strength to strength and can now be found at about a dozen locations across Sydney. Star Café Wash has created a new car wash category—it is a cafe with a car wash attached to it. You can either go there to get your car washed or you can just stop in for a coffee and some cafe fare. Unlike other car wash companies you don't just get a free cup of coffee when you get your car washed, you can visit the cafe and have a Simmone Logue sandwich, a New Zealand Natural ice-cream or the best espresso in the area. Star Café Wash is now a very successful brand that has found its own niche and created its own category.

To use an example from another industry, I have also worked with a group of landscape gardeners who have created their own category based around 'total works'. Most landscapers will mow your lawn, trim the shrubs, lay down some mulch or bring in some new plants. This company, however, can also build a 100 acre wetland, a road or a small building—that is, it takes care of the whole works. It is hoped that with time the concept of 'total works' will become part of the vocabulary of developers and builders, which will only cement their position.

In a product sense, a good example of the development of a new category is Ice Magic. Cottee's, the company behind the product, wanted to create a chocolate topping that went hard when poured on ice-cream. Ice Magic was the result and has been an enormous success for the company. To this day Cottee's still owns this category.

In their book *Chasing Cool*, authors Noah Kerner and Gene Pressman discuss the creation of the perception of and category for the premium vodka Grey Goose. The developer of Grey Goose broke with a number of traditions by designing a French premium vodka. He presented Grey Goose in a smoked glass bottle housed in wooden box. The price point, the packaging, the presentation and the whole vibe around Grey Goose was 'premium'. He then positioned Grey Goose as being the world's best-tasting vodka. The interesting fact is that in blind taste tests Absolut Vodka actually won on every front for taste. Even with these results, because of the positioning and vibe of Grey Goose, it has been placed at the top of the category both in perception and price.

Brand building today is often a battle of categories, not a battle of promotion.

Even iconic personalities can create a category. Donald Trump has created his own category on the Manhattan real estate landscape, all under the Trump brand.

If you create a category, you must create an awareness of that category in the mind of your target audience, and then fulfil the promise that has them recognising their own need for that category. As Gary Hamel and CK Prahalad commented in their book *Competing for the Future*, 'Some companies ask customers what they want. Market leaders know what customers want before customers know themselves'. The outcome is that you instantly become the market leader in this new category. Brand building today is often a battle of categories, not a battle of promotion.

Repeat, repeat, repeat

Once you have decided on your category, the word you own and your positioning statement, you must then use it constantly. Importantly, it's not about how much money you spend, it's about hitting your customer with your positioning statement in *every* communication. You can't over-communicate your positioning.

Woolworths supermarkets is a classic example. For about 25 years Woolworths has convinced grocery buyers that Woolworths is the fresh food people. It even has a 'Fresh Food Kids' promotion, which includes a charity sponsorship called the Fresh Food Kids Hospital Appeal and the Fresh Food Kids Community Grants Program. In the promotional material for its Everyday Money Credit Card, the headline read: 'Switch now and start earning shopping cards. The credit card fresh from Woolworths'. Woolworths 'fresh food people' signage is the first thing you see when you walk into the stores, it's on its trucks, on staff uniforms and in its television advertising. The company also has a magazine, which is called *Fresh,* and it also does 'fresh' market reports during newsbreaks. Its positioning statement is also on the front page and throughout its annual report, which communicates the message to its shareholders. Woolworths is an excellent example of 'repeat, repeat, repeat', and it has reaped the rewards as a result. This is the reason I'm pretty sure you wouldn't have been able to tell me what Coles' positioning statement is! (At the time of writing, it's 'It all counts'.)

Brand building can have a compounding effect, much like the way regular deposits have a compounding effect on your bank balance over time. Just like putting money regularly into the bank over time, the longer you leave it in there, the more money you will make. The more often your target audience is exposed to your positioning statement, the greater the equity in your brand. The more you use it, the more brand recognition you get. The great thing about this strategy is that you don't need to spend any extra money to communicate your statement. You can do exactly what you're already doing, just do it better. Examples of where you can use your positioning statement include letterhead, invoices, flyers, company profiles, tender documents, signage, email signatures, each page of your website, induction documents, recruitment documents, rewards programs, the lunch room, dispatch signs, banners, conference displays, packaging and point of sale. Repeat, repeat, repeat and take advantage of the compounding value of your brand.

Never change your positioning statement

Once you've decided on your positioning statement, don't ever change it. It should remain in place forever. This is why Woolworths, David Jones and Qantas have had such great success cementing their brands in the public consciousness. When you look at their main competitors—Coles, Myer and some of the other Australian airlines—all of them change their positioning almost yearly, which explains why we can't recite their statements now.

Mortein's 'Louie the fly', Antz Pantz's 'Sick 'em Rex', Razzamatazz's 'Uh oh, Razzamatazz' and Pea Beau's 'Hit 'em high, hit 'em low, hit 'em with the old Pea Beau' are all campaigns that made a resurgence in the early 2000s. I imagine the story goes something like this: a new marketing or brand manager comes on board and, in order to prove him or herself, dumps the old positioning and creates a new one with a hired agency. Before the manager knows it the company has been through four different positionings, so he or she decides to undertake market research with the target audience. The target audience recounts the great campaigns of five, 10 or 15 years ago when the brand was strong and owned a perception, and lo and behold the marketer decides to reintroduce the positioning statement the company never should have left in the first place! Don't be tempted to continually change your positioning. Take the time to think, strategise and implement well, and your positioning will last a lifetime.

Don't be tempted to continually change your positioning.

I know some of you might be thinking that times change and so does your target audience. That may be so, but your positioning should still stay the same—you just need to execute it differently. 'There's no other store like David Jones' is different today from when my mum shopped there back in the 1970s. The designers and the food are different, the homewares and accessories are all different, but the overall position is the same. Back then it might have been 'There's no other store like David Jones for Carla Zampatti', but today it's 'For Sass & Bide, there's no other store like David Jones'. The positioning remains the same, it's the tactics, imaging and story that change.

Things to remember

It's time now to move on to the next step in the process of building your brand—and that is bringing all the elements covered in this chapter together to begin generating a vibe for your brand.

Start with the fundamentals

A lot of this chapter may seem pretty straightforward and simple, but it's surprising how few people get the fundamentals right. I've worked with some of the biggest and best companies in Australia and overseas, and when you pull these organisations back to the fundamentals, it's amazing how easy it is to identify the gaps in their marketing model.

Take, for example, the day I worked with one of Australia's biggest brewers. Just before the morning break I asked the group whether there were any particular questions they would like to discuss and a young strategist, Jeremy, put up his hand and said, 'I've just got one question, why should I buy your beer?' From the awkward silence that followed it was obvious that the group couldn't clearly articulate in one sentence why anyone should buy their beer. I tended to agree with Jeremy when he said, 'We should probably start there today'.

Remember, it comes down to working out the following:

- who you are talking to
- what you do

➽ why people should buy from you

➽ how you are going to tell people about it.

Here is an example of a well-articulated marketing model:

➽ *Name*: Star Café Wash.

➽ *Target*: couples who care about their vehicles.

➽ *Product*: cafe and car wash.

➽ *Category*: cafe wash.

➽ *Word to own*: best.

➽ *Position*: 'The best wash is a Star Wash'.

➽ *Promotion*: flyers, text messaging, online, membership cards and so on.

If you take away all of the bells and whistles and just get the fundamentals right, you will be well on your way to success.

Keep it simple

One of the reasons people find it so hard to articulate what they do is because they do so many different things. Today, with management teams and shareholders expecting 15 to 20 per cent growth year after year, companies automatically look for new angles, product extensions or product developments to stimulate growth. They confuse capabilities with true brand perception. Sometimes when you try to add additional capabilities to your brand, you unwittingly erode what you're 'famous' for.

For example, US antacid medicine Alka-Seltzer was always known for its fizzy taste, but when it tried to do a cough mixture it failed. A lot of surf-wear labels are unable to successfully sell surfboards because they're famous for clothes not boards. Some skate-board clothing manufacturers can't 'do' skateboards, while some skateboard *... success is not based on whether you can or can't come up with a new product...* manufacturers can do clothing. Remember, success is not based on whether you can or can't come up with a new product; it's based on whether perceptually your target audience will 'get it' and allow you to or not.

Cenovis was famous for its multivitamins in tablet form, but when it moved into Cenovis fizzy vitamins it failed because that was territory held by Berocca. When Starbucks tried to retail a range of soft furnishings from its stores, it failed as Starbucks is famous for its coffee not soft furnishings. Interestingly, however, Starbucks has won six Grammy awards and is one of the biggest sellers of music in the world. Perceptually, according to Starbucks's customers, they're happy to buy music played and stocked at Starbucks, but not soft furnishings. Once again, it's not whether you can try something new or not, it's just perceptually whether your audience will wear it or not.

Another good example is Kit Kat. When Kit Kat decided to sell mint-flavoured Kit Kats the consumer didn't buy them. Mint Slice held the consumer's perception of a mint-flavoured chocolate snack. Then when Kit Kat tried to sell a Kit Kat biscuit, it came up against Tim Tams, the market leader in chocolate biscuits. I remember sitting with the Kit Kat team at Nestlé and asking them what had happened to those two products. They told me they realised Kit Kat was a chocolate, not a biscuit. How far you can push your brand depends entirely on the perception in the mind of your target audience.

The process of deciding whether your target will allow you to push the brand is in most cases largely common sense. When Milky Way created a Tutti-Frutti Milky Way it was destined for failure. When I present to audiences and mention the words Tutti-Frutti Milky Way people's faces screw up as they try to imagine a citrus-flavoured milk product.

If you want to move into a new area for your brand or create a new product to extend the bottom line in your organisation, then you may want to consider the strategy successfully used by a number of companies. Toyota, for example, distributes and sells the Lexus brand of luxury car. It has built on one perception and used a separate brand with separate dealerships and a separate vibe to meet that need. Nutella is another example. It's famous as a hazelnut-based spread and forms part of the Ferrero Rocher family, yet no-one ever confuses Nutella with Ferrero Rocher premium chocolates. Although they come from the same company, they are two separate products with two separate marketing models and a separate vibe for each. In fact, you have to look very closely at a Nutella bottle to even see the Ferrero Rocher name in the address of the manufacturer.

Kleenex has done the same thing with its portfolio of toilet tissue. Kleenex, Cottonelle and Viva are all part of the Kleenex stable, yet each has its own position and perception in the marketplace. This is a clever strategy to try to cover all price points and perceptual angles for consumers no matter what level of entry they have going into the market.

An accounting firm that I came across became a specialist in banks and insolvency, but it also had a bookkeeping division. The bookkeeping division never gained any real foothold in the marketplace, even though the firm gave it priority and continually talked to its existing customers about it. What it realised was that it was seen as a specialist in banking and insolvency, but not in bookkeeping. Consequently, the firm created a separate brand for the bookkeeping division, with a separate team and a completely different identity and vibe—that is, it had a different brand name, positioning and office structure. The bookkeeping division is now growing at a great rate.

Deliver on your promise

Now you've identified your target audience and can articulate specifically what you do, you've worked out what position you want to own in the mind of your target audience and you've started to promote it, there's one last thing to think about. If you can't deliver on the perception that you are creating in the mind of your target audience, then you're on a road to nowhere. It's like putting lipstick on a pig—you're dressing it up, but it's still a pig. You must be able to deliver on your promise.

A great example of this is Ribena blackcurrant fruit drink. For many years Ribena had been promoting that if you drank a glass a day, it would make up a substantial part of your daily vitamin C intake. However, in 2004 during a school science experiment two students from New Zealand found that their ready-to-drink Ribena contained almost no trace of vitamin C. This discovery clearly contradicted Ribena's promise, and as a result Ribena's parent company was fined and the Ribena brand will take a long time to recover. Why? Because the company had spent a great deal of time, energy and money creating a perception that proved to be false. Even though the company later came out and claimed that its advertising was a misrepresentation, it was too late, the damage had already been done. Marketing at its core is not based on reality, it's all about perception. Although the product had not changed, Ribena almost overnight went from having a great vibe to a really poor vibe due to perception about the product.

You need to fully involve your people in the marketing and position of the brand.

Getting started

It's time now to begin creating a vibe for your company, product or service. Here are the steps you need to take to do so.

Step 1: decide the word you want to own

The first step is to choose the word you want to own. Build a positioning statement around it that will be presented with your logo everywhere that it appears. The phrase and the logo should be on your letterhead, your emails, your website, the sides of your trucks, banners, posters, trade-show displays, flyers, recruitment announcements, training documents, internal memos, trade magazines, on the radio, on the television and in the press. Wherever your logo appears, so must your positioning.

Step 2: tell your team

Once you have decided on the word you want to own and you've built your phrase, you then need to tell your team. Everyone in the whole organisation needs to understand your positioning, the word you want to own and who your target market is. Make an announcement to your team and then use your positioning statement everywhere. Do an internal and an external audit and use it at every opportunity. Remember, you can't over-communicate your phrase.

Step 3: engage your people

You need to fully involve your people in the marketing and position of the brand. It's one thing to tell your team about the marketing and position of the brand, but you must get them to live it. This is done by catching them using it, by constant reinforcement, by holding the senior management accountable for the delivery of the word and its promise to create the perception.

Step 4: constantly repeat your position

You need to sell your position through everything you do. The only way to truly cement your word into the mind of your team and your customers or clients is through repetition. Every time you have contact with a customer or client you must sell your position—that is, your message. It's the consistency of doing this that builds the position, but it's the repetition that builds your brand.

Don't fall into the random acts of marketing trap. You build sales in the short term, but you build brands over the long term. A brand is like having a term deposit in the bank. It's the compounding interest or effect of the repetition of your message that builds your brand. It takes years to build a strong brand with an unbreakable perception. But it's the compounding effect over time of every brochure, conversation, flyer, the website, the email address and the comment over coffee with your client or customer that reinforces itself to build a perception.

Vibe status

- ⏵ Have you worked out who the target for your product or service is?

- ⏵ Can you articulate what your company, product or service is in one sentence?

❯ Do you own a word?

❯ Do you need to create your own category?

❯ Does everyone in your organisation know your positioning statement and who your target market is?

❯ Are you promoting your positioning statement? Are you creating a perception in the mind of your target market?

❯ Are you delivering on your promise?

Chapter 2

Raise the roof on your brand

In 2007 it was reported on CNN that Coca-Cola was worth a staggering US$67 billion. Similar figures were also thrown around for some of the world's biggest and most recognised brands such as Marlboro, McDonald's, Disney and De Beers. I believe there are a number of important lessons we can learn from these companies that we can apply to our own businesses, regardless of their size, to help them evolve into the brands we envisage them to be. Today, we have the first-ever US$100 billion brand. Can you guess who? Yep, it's Google (and it took the company just over 10 years to reach this milestone!).

In this chapter I'll explain what you can do to raise the roof on your brand—that is, how to make it recognisable and continue building a vibe around it, and turn it into the brand you want it to be. This chapter is not about learning how to be the biggest or most successful company in the marketplace, it's just about being your best. By aiming to be the very best you can be, your thinking changes and it is this change in thinking that will enable you to take your business to the next level, and will set you on a path to managing an outstanding brand.

Create a vision for your brand

To begin the chapter I would like to discuss the importance of creating a vision of where you wish to take your brand in the future. The creators of brands such as Dell Computers, Virgin, Disney and Jimmy Choo all started with a vision of where they wanted to take their brand. That is not to say that these brands were conceived with strategic or brand plans securely in place or that along the way there weren't mistakes made, obstacles to overcome and adjustments made. However, their creators certainly had a clear picture in their mind of what they wanted to do and/or achieve with their business, and they stayed true to that vision.

If you are the leader or owner of a brand, what is your vision for your brand five or 10 years down the track? If you have a clearly articulated picture in your mind, then you are already halfway to achieving that vision.

Remember, you get what you focus on. Articulating exactly where you'd like your brand to be in five, 10, 15 or 20 years' time, and not straying from that vision, has great power. I spoke on this very topic to the senior management team of an Adelaide-based supermarket chain, and was fortunate enough to be present when the owner of the business (who was in his mid 60s at the time), stood in front of his team and said, 'In 20 years' time our brand will be ... ', and

Articulating exactly where you'd like your brand to be ... and not straying from that vision has great power.

proceeded to outline his vision for the brand. It gave me goose bumps and great faith in the future of the company that its owner could so clearly articulate a vision for the company that far into the future.

Specifically, what I'm talking about is an individual brand vision, which can be quite different from your company vision, as a company may own several brands. For example, Mars Incorporated is one of the largest food manufacturers in the world and operates as six different business segments—chocolate, pet care, chewing gum, food, drinks and symbioscience. Its brands include M&M's, Snickers, Dove, Mars, Extra and Orbit, as well as the pet care brands Pedigree, Royal Canin and Whiskas. In addition, Mars owns the Masterfoods range. Each of these brands will have its own marketing model and brand plan complete with individual targets, category development, positioning statements and so on. Simply by having an individual vision you know in which direction you're heading.

It seems that even in human resources you need to be able to articulate a vision for your brand. Peter Sheahan, a well-respected author and keynote speaker who is an expert on what the new generation thinks about employment and branding, notes the tendency of generation Y to interview you and your company when seeking employment rather than the other way around. Interestingly, it seems this generation wants to know what you as an organisation do, what you're giving back to society and where the brand is going to be in five or 10 years' time. In the back of their minds they are evaluating how well they think they will fit into that vision. If you recruit staff yourself you may already be aware of this trend. If not, it is an interesting discussion to have with someone in the industry!

Whether in good times or bad, you shouldn't just manage a brand, you have to lead it, and you can't lead a brand unless you have a vision for where the brand is going. Let me use the following analogy of the Koi fish. If kept in a goldfish bowl a Koi will remain the size of a goldfish. If you put it into a large birdbath, then it will grow larger to fit its larger environment. If, however, you put the Koi in lush wetlands, then it can grow to between one and two feet long! As with the Koi, a brand grows in accordance with the vision that the leader has for it. Are you currently confining your brand to a goldfish bowl? Are you willing to let it flourish in the wetlands?

Are you holding back your brand?

I have found that many CEOs, managing directors or brand managers put limits on the quality and/or the

standards that they set for their brand and its future.
I regularly hear comments such as 'We don't have the
money', 'We're only a small Australian company', 'We
work in the manufacturing industry' or 'We're just
accountants'. All these negative thoughts (or ceilings, as I
like to refer to them) put limits on what these individuals
believe is possible for their brand. I like to challenge
them to be more entrepreneurial and recognise that by
removing these ceilings there is great opportunity for
growth and truly raising the roof on your brand. Don't
hold back your brand by focusing on negative thoughts.
Remember, one person's ceiling is another person's floor!
Figure 2.1 illustrates my concept of raising the roof on
your brand.

Figure 2.1: raise the roof on your brand

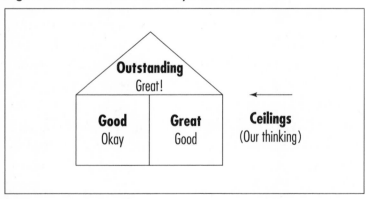

In any category, whether it's shampoo, taxation, beer
or television antennas, there will always be a group of
companies competing for your dollar. In any category,
there will be myriad companies doing a fair or good job.
Sure they'll deliver, but they'll deliver only as much as

they have to, to get the sale. These are the brands doing a good job and they'll get the okay sales rewards.

Also, in any category there will be some brands that are doing a great job. These are the brands that deliver on time every time and even perhaps offer a few little extras for your dollar. These great brands will consistently achieve the good results, get good sales and attract good people.

Yet in every category there will always be one brand that stands out—that is, there will be an outstanding shampoo brand, an outstanding television antenna company or an outstanding publishing house. These outstanding brands achieve great results. These brands attract the best people (as I tend to say, 'stars' want to work for 'stars') and receive the greatest rewards. What separates the outstanding from the good and the great is essentially just thinking.

What separates the outstanding from the good and the great is essentially just thinking.

The outstanding brands set a vision for themselves—they don't have ceilings, they have floors. They don't settle for good brochures, they want outstanding brochures. They don't have a good website, they have an outstanding website. They don't want good or great workers, they want the truly outstanding workers. These people set a standard that is reflected in everything to do with their brand(s). Their advertising, their people, their service, their hospitality— everything is reflected in the positive vibe of the brand.

I recently read a blog by author Seth Godin, a marketing and brand ambassador, and someone who 'walks the talk'. On the subject of mediocrity, he commented:

> Doing 4 per cent less does not get you 4 per cent less. Doing 4 per cent less may very well get you 95 per cent less. That's because almost good enough gets you nowhere. No sales, no votes, no customers. The sad lie of mediocrity is the mistaken belief that partial effort yields partial results. In fact the results are usually totally out of proportion to the incremental effort.

I couldn't agree more. To raise the roof on your brand you must remove the ceilings—the thinking—that are holding you back. For those who say, 'We don't have the budget', I say to them that it's not a budget thing, it's a thinking thing. Those people who say, 'We're only a small company here in the back blocks of Brisbane, we could never be like that', that's a ceiling. All companies start small, but it is the leaders who have a vision, who set the standard and ultimately set themselves on a path to achieving their dreams. That doesn't necessarily mean they are aiming for their company to be the largest or the leader, or being global, it just means that you as a brand set yourself the challenge of being outstanding in everything you do—that is, in your presentation, your people, your message and your follow-through all must be world class. It is this thinking that will result in you becoming an outstanding brand.

Seth Godin, in his book *The Dip*, says that if you're not holding yourself to world-class standards, then you're essentially just white space. If you are the same as everyone else in your category, then you will just disappear. Only a small percentage of brands in any category make the 'outstanding' grade, but no matter which category you happen to be in, there's always a brand that is head and shoulders above the rest. These outstanding brands often have market share that is three, five or even 10 times greater than their nearest competitor.

Do you know whose vision it was to be the biggest retailer in the world? It was Jeff Bezos from Amazon, someone who keeps working despite the incredible success of his brand. On a smaller scale, I worked with an Australian recruitment CEO in his 30s who is also an information technology whiz. The vision he has for his recruitment company is to revolutionise recruitment globally through his innovative IT platform. Another client I worked with in Melbourne has a vision to be in every bathroom throughout Australia. A service-based company that I worked with in Sydney has a vision of redefining their industry. I recently received the annual report for a credit union in Adelaide called Savings & Loans. Its vision is to be the best member-owned financial institution for everyday Australians. It's been a pleasure watching this organisation go from strength to strength over the last five to seven years up against the larger banks. One of my favourites is the accounting firm in Brisbane I mentioned earlier. It has a stated vision of being the most recognised accounting brand worldwide in providing entrepreneurial success.

From the very beginning the vision for the brand Jimmy Choo was to become a global women's luxury accessory brand. The brand featured heavily in the television show *Sex and the City* and is currently one of the most sought-after shoe brands in the world. In a stepped process,

40 per cent of Jimmy Choo's turnover now comes from handbags and it has brought out a range of sunglasses. But it all started with a vision, a set of standards and a belief in the brand. If you can't see where your brand will be down the track, then it's time to get your troops together and work it out. Remember, this is a brand vision not a company vision. If the company name happens to be the brand name, however, then they can be the same thing. I truly believe that if you can visualise the end result, you can make it happen.

... if you can visualise the end result, you can make it happen.

Another more recent example of brand vision that I think is worth considering is the vision for Scribd, the largest social publishing company in the world. It's a website that more than 60 million people use each month to discover and share original written work. When they started, their vision for the business was 'deliberate the written word'—how cool!

One of the more exciting brands I've seen in many years is a UK ice-cream boutique, called The Icecreamists. Its vision is 'To liberate the world from ordinary ice-cream one lick at a time'. One look at its website and you will see why these guys really have created a category all of their own, a real rock-and-roll form of ice-cream! Working with companies large and small on a daily basis, it doesn't take long to gauge whether the creator and/or senior management team have any vision for the future. Does your company have something that is driving it or are you doing the same old thing?

So many Australian companies that I work with don't hold themselves to world-class standards, and I find this fascinating. They seem to believe they can't compete on a world stage for whatever reason (whether budgetary, geographical and so on), but as I remind them, this way of thinking is just a ceiling to their future growth. In fact, the world of marketing and branding is changing at an increasingly rapid rate and your thinking really needs to reflect this. Something that you believe is not even applicable to your particular company or industry may affect it more than you could ever imagine over time. Take, for example, the way things have changed in the world of street directories. These days you can get directions from your mobile phone along with restaurant information, bank locations, service stations and red-light cameras. So much for the printed directory you used to have in your car!

Someone who never let himself be held back is Australia's king of cosmetics, Napoleon Perdis. In his own words, he was just a Greek kid living in Melbourne who had a vision of creating an international cosmetics brand, who dreamt of having a store on Fifth Avenue and his own private jet. He now has his Fifth Avenue store, a global brand and I'd say he's well on his way to having his own private jet. The lesson: create a vision, take away the ceilings and dream big. In an increasingly interconnected world and a global marketplace, can you really afford not to?

If you put ceilings over your brand you're going to be left behind, and, ultimately, you may end up damaging the very brand you're trying so hard to build. Everything about you, your brand and how you do things needs to be of a world-class standard. Indeed, writer William Somerset Maugham observed, 'It's a funny thing about life; if you refuse to accept anything but the best, you quite often get it'. But I want to reiterate, success is not a money thing, it's a thinking thing, and if you change your thinking, you can achieve your vision, whatever that may be and on whatever budget.

What is outstanding? How great do you have to be?

What will it take for your brand to be the best in its category? What would it take for you to have world-class standards for your brand in your category? Are you up for it? As I noted earlier, to be outstanding essentially means to stand out. You must aim to stand out from everyone else in every aspect of your brand portfolio. It's the little things done well that elevate a brand to the status of outstanding and put it above the 'white space'.

Once again, it's about your thinking and your attitude. To win Wimbledon, a tennis player only has to win one more point than his or her opponent. In horse racing the Melbourne Cup winner only has win by a nose. The winners of the Melbourne Cup are remembered for generations—can you say the same for the horses that came second? In the Olympics an athlete can win the 100 metre sprint by less than one hundredth of a second—that's not much in my books! Tiger Woods only has to sink one less shot than his opponent to win the US Masters and go into the record books. As the winner you will be remembered, while the second, third or fourth placegetters tend to be difficult to recollect, if they are remembered at all.

In 2007 I met Paul Cave, who successfully established the Sydney Harbour Bridge Climb, one of the must-see attractions in Sydney. When Paul started his business he had clear vision for it. He wanted the Sydney Harbour Bridge Climb to be 'the world's best attraction, every climb, every time'. It may have taken Paul 10 years of challenges and setbacks to get that first person to the top of the bridge, but through it all he refused to put ceilings over his vision. Anyone who's done the bridge climb would have to agree that his vision has been achieved — every climb, every time. Remember, it's pretty hard to win against a competitor who has an outstanding vibe!

... it's essential to surround yourself with the right people ...

Set up a brand council

As I've mentioned, to be outstanding you just need to stand out. However, as a leader of a brand you can't do it on your own. In order to be truly outstanding it's essential to surround yourself with the right people who will help you achieve that standard — to create what I like to call your brand council.

Whether you are a small organisation or a large multi-national, it is important to establish a council and set regular meetings where you listen and strategise about past activities and future plans. Your council can be a wonderful springboard to challenge your thinking and break some of the habitual practices of your organisation. It has been said that if you always do what you've always done, you always get what you've always got, and with the increasing pace of change in today's world, it won't be good enough tomorrow.

So who should be on your brand council? This is quite a subjective question and differs depending on your resource base. Your brand council might consist of your CEO, CFO, sales director, marketing manager, perhaps an outside consultant and/or even a couple of young sales or operations people who are passionate about the brand and who have good common sense and an ability to think strategically about your market. During these strategy sessions you will need to consider your competitors, their positioning, the perception they carry and tactically what they are doing to promote themselves.

If you're a smaller organisation and not fortunate enough to have these types of numbers, then you may need to use outside mentors who can provide valuable insight, an unbiased opinion and who can perhaps offer suggestions from different categories that are unrelated to yours. Occasionally, I am asked to attend a brand council meeting for a client and for a couple of hours I'm able to bring a perspective from outside their own industry, as well as cast an unbiased set of eyes across their planning and execution. I also know CEOs of a number of companies that target female audiences, who have asked their wives to form part of their council. Other marketers from smaller organisations I know have their brother and/or sister as part of their council, as they may have a close association with the target audience.

Whatever the make-up of your council, it's imperative that each member has a desire and passion to contribute to the success of your brand through good times and bad. Everyone is happy to be a part of a brand when things are good, but it's when times are tough and the ship is sinking that everyone runs for the lifeboats. The true character of your council will come during those tough times. Film director Stephen Spielberg, during his acceptance speech of the Cecil B DeMille Lifetime Achievement Award at the 2009 Golden Globes, thanked his mentor, Sid Sheinberg, the former head of Universal Studios who had been a mentor to Spielberg since the age of 22. One of the things that Sheinberg apparently said to Spielberg in the early days of their friendship that resonated with him was, 'I'll always be there for you in success, but I'll also always be there for you through the tough times'.

In your organisation, if you are fortunate to have the numbers, I suggest that you gather your brand council together once a quarter or once every six months to strategise. When I worked in radio our brand council would meet at a particular radio station every three months, where we'd look at what we had done for the last three months and strategise for the months ahead. We would analyse research to understand how listeners felt about the radio station. This was our brand council and we considered our quarterly get-togethers to be our war room.

Included in our brand council were the program director, promotions director, group program director, sales director, the station's general manager, the research director and sometimes even a consultant from overseas. The sales director was present because she was in touch with clients and also once the strategy was set she had the responsibility of selling it to our clients. The promotions, programming and research teams were there to strategise the positioning of the radio station in the marketplace,

... gather your brand council together once a quarter or once every six months ...

look at how our competitors were positioned, where they were moving with their strategy and to think about what their next step might be. The general manager was there to keep the peace and make sure that all parties were being fair and equitable to drive the brand forward. The consultant brought us new trends and new perspectives from outside the market and quite often just kept us honest. The importance of a brand council for me is summed up in a quote from HE Luccock, who said, 'No-one can whistle a symphony. It takes an orchestra to play it'.

Create a vibe inside your organisation

There is a relatively new term in marketing and branding, which is 'employer branding'. Will Ruch, CEO and managing partner of US company Versant and leading authority on employer branding, defines employer branding as the image of a brand as seen through the eyes of its associates and potential hires. Earlier in the book I suggested performing an internal and external audit of your marketing material. As part of your internal audit, ask yourself whether the position and perception you want to create in the mind of your target audience is part of the DNA of your organisation. Pull out your last couple of recruitment ads, your induction manual, your quarterly reviews, your employee performance surveys, your sales meeting minutes, your national conference agenda and anything else that you use as a means to communicate your culture, standards, company direction or brand to your internal team. If your employees don't understand what makes the company special, what it's striving for, and what perception it's trying to create in the mind of the target audience, then how are they possibly to know their responsibility in helping to deliver the dream?

It's as much about creating a vibe inside the organisation with your people as it is about selling the vibe to your customers. It should be embedded in your company in the same way that you would hope to embed the mission, vision and values of your business. It's surprising how often internal staff are overlooked. It's the team members who will deliver your brand promise. It's the thinking of the team that will set the standards and ultimately execute your plans. Indeed, as America's Cup skipper Dennis Connor has noted, 'Once your direction becomes clear to you and fully visible to others, all elements of winning—attitude, performance, teamwork and competition—begin to come together'.

There does need a bit of creativity applied to how you will sell the message to your team and how you will measure it. Consider figure 2.2. You need to have a marketing plan for your staff, as well as customers or clients.

Figure 2.2: three-way brand engagement

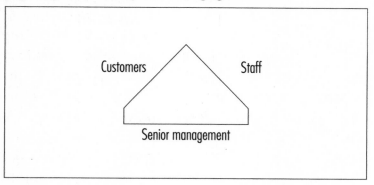

There are many different ways you can market internally to your team. There are the traditional screensavers, mouse pads, signage around the buildings, T-shirts or presentations by the marketing or senior management team, but just remember that it's all these things and more, done on a consistent basis over a long period of time, that is the way to embed a positioning statement into your employees' minds. You need to do it exactly the same way as you do with your customers—through repetition. Simply mounting a large banner or sign on the factory wall won't do, as after two weeks that sign becomes wallpaper and people don't notice it anymore.

You constantly need to find new and interesting ways to engage your team in your marketing process.

Not only do you need to repeat your positioning at every meeting, you also need to actively measure it and reward it to make it stick. I know of a CEO of a manufacturing company whose positioning is 'The mark of reliability'. If this company was hiring staff, it could begin that employee's induction into its internal marketing by stating in the recruitment ad that the company is seeking the most 'reliable' person in the city to work in the business. If you're trying to decide between two potential recruits, each one should be asked to justify his or her level of reliability—instances when they have been reliable in the past and how they will be reliable for you. At the company's Christmas party they decided to create a 'mark of reliability' in the form of a trophy that was presented to team members who had consistently demonstrated reliability in one way or another, either internally or externally, over the course of the year. It starts there and then is embedded in the corporate culture through repetition in all aspects of the business.

... market to your senior management team.

One other important point is to market to your senior management team. If the management team doesn't adopt and live out your positioning statement, then you can't expect anyone else in the organisation to do so. You must consistently revisit it through your own management teams, planning sessions, strategic conferences and national get-togethers. If you're a one-off or a sole operator, then make a note in your diary that once every three months you'll take a morning to sit in a coffee shop, look at your materials and examine your competitors. This would also be a good time for you to sit with a mentor or part of your brand council to help critique your marketing and to fire off ideas and challenge you for the months ahead.

Vibe status

> Do you have a vision for your brand?

> Is your thinking holding back your brand?

> Do you hold yourself to world-class standards?

> Does the executive team that is driving the brand know the vision?

> Does your brand stand out from all the others in its category?

> Have you established a brand council?

Chapter 3

The changing face of branding

The word cloud surrounding the chapter title includes: ervation, category, brands, generous, create, trends, thinking, community, position, company, defining, ceilings, better, Apple, client, awareness, customers, loyalty, fundamentals, mind, need, people, ness story, successful, think, misation, creating, vision, sensory, marketi, manager, websites, audience, Woolwo, different, Twitter, communicate, listen, money, vibe, different, business, question, time, growth, review, media

In an increasingly sophisticated marketplace, everything about branding is changing—your relationship with customers, your marketing, your promotion, all the way through to the way your brand is perceived. Today's brands operate in an ever-changing environment. In this chapter we will explore current trends that exist in branding, as well as ways of keeping up with those changes.

See what's around you

Before we go any further I need to ask you one question: given the dramatic rate at which branding is changing, are you walking around with your eyes and ears open to even notice these changes? Traditional marketers such as John Saunders of Westfield or Sam Walton of US chain Walmart used to regularly walk around their stores and talk and listen to their target audience to find out what problems they could solve for them. They were classically trained marketers who walked the floor with their eyes and ears open to seize any opportunity to enhance their brand. This observational skill is something that is as essential today as it was in years past, and if you can master this skill as a marketer, you open up a wealth of possibilities for you and your brand. If you simply have your eyes and ears open when you're talking to friends, sitting in coffee shops, reading magazines, sitting on board an aeroplane, shopping in department stores or watching television, then you are able to see what other people choose not to, and this is where a great marketer can really excel. It is the marketer and the brand manager who can see these things and think differently about how they go to market, present their brand and fix their target's problems, who are the success stories of the future.

When Andrew Denton interviewed comedian Jerry Seinfeld on the ABC television series *Enough Rope*, he asked him whether, as an observational comedian, he had to train himself to observe what was going on around him. Seinfeld responded that he just picks things out as they go by and thinks maybe he could do something with that. Unfortunately today too many people walk around with their eyes locked firmly to the ground or to their phones checking emails and sending text messages. Whether or not you work in a marketing department, observation is a great asset to possess. If you're a marketing or branding person, it's a fantastic skill to foster. By training yourself to walk around with your eyes and ears open you expose yourself to a whole world of trends and goings on that could be used by your brand.

When I was working with a group of bankers in 2009, I asked them to make a list of recent trends that they had observed among their friends, family and colleagues. They soon had a list built around communication, health, nutrition, lifestyle and interaction. Then I asked the bankers what they were doing about their observations. At this point I was met with blank stares and one person actually said, 'What do you mean? These have nothing to do with banking!' I pointed out that the group was creating a ceiling by thinking they had to see and do things in a certain way in keeping with other financial institutions.

If you're a marketing or branding person, [observation is] a great skill to foster.

One of the trends the group had noticed was colour —specifically fluorescent colour. When I asked the group to throw ideas around about how they could take advantage of this colour trend through their point of sale, uniforms, branches and website, the penny started to drop. The next trend they discussed was the move into new media, including MP3 players, iPhones, BlackBerries, and audio and video podcasts, and we talked about how these things could be used to help their customers. As we worked through the list of trends you could almost see the ideas being generated in the minds of these eager young marketers as they started to understand the scope of possibility that had suddenly been presented to them.

In a blog he posted in 2009, titled 'When you notice it, it's news', Seth Godin wrote about an article he had read discussing how some musicians were reporting that their perfect pitch (the ability to know what a perfect C sounds like) was fading away, and what might be causing this. Seth commented that he didn't think that there was anything in particular causing this loss, and that it's difficult to imagine that throughout history, a small proportion of musicians had not lost their perfect pitch. The difference is that in the old days no-one heard about it. Word didn't spread. He went on to explain that as word about your product or brand spreads, it bumps into other news and becomes a trend, thus what had begun as an opinion piece about perfect pitch suddenly became news to a global audience.

Seth's blog raises two points. Firstly, someone had to notice the trend, and then someone else had to do something about it. By doing this your customers or clients will be thankful because they will know that you are the person who was seeing things differently. Secondly, information is spreading so quickly that a good vibe or a bad vibe can spread faster than ever before. If you don't deliver on your promise or you start to fade into the white space of mediocrity, word will quickly spread and that can have a lasting effect on the value of your brand. Good vibes are compounding and must be built, whereas a bad vibe will spread like a bushfire and quickly erode your brand.

What's your story?

I hope that by now you have had a chance to work through your marketing model and you understand the basic principles, and you're beginning to realise that the vibe is more than just those marketing materials. The vibe is also about building an authentic story that helps contribute to a positive perception about your brand. It's about marketing your story internally and externally, and it's about being more than just a brand to your customer.

The vibe is also about building an authentic story...

Authenticity is a trend that is currently sweeping the world, and as a marketer it is an important one to be aware of. Consumers are showing a preference for ethical, authentic products with a real story rather than over-marketed commercial products. They want to know what the product is about, where it comes from and why they should be a part of your community. It's worth remembering, however, that today's consumer is fairly sophisticated and won't be fooled easily, and is also perhaps more fickle then ever before. When today's consumers speak they expect the whole world to be listening. If they don't like what they see, they can also tell the world in just two clicks. With the average attention span of today's consumers at about 10 seconds, you also need to be able to capture people's imaginations quickly. The easiest and quickest way to deliver true authenticity is to develop and then share the story of your brand. I'll illustrate what I mean with some examples of successful brands that have a great story.

The Moleskine notebook is a wonderful example. Moleskine notebooks have reportedly held the inspirations and ideas of everyone from Van Gogh, Picasso and Hemmingway to famed author Bruce Chapman. Artists, authors and geniuses of all varieties have long appreciated the simplicity and superior functionality of these notebooks, and this is the story told on the Moleskine website.

Another one of my favourites is Nudie fruit juice drinks. The Nudie story is now quite familiar to Australians and New Zealanders, but for those who don't know the story behind the brand, here it is as told on its website:

> Tall Tim loved fresh juices and fruit crushes and smoothies (we call him Tall Tim because he's tall and his name is Tim). But Tall Tim didn't always have time to make his own and no one else would make it for him. So Tim got to thinking, there must be a lot of other people just like him (though not as tall). So Tim did some in-depth research. He asked some friends if they liked fresh smoothies and fruit juices and crushes with nothing else added. Their answer was yes and the rest is history.

The style of the piece is typical of the quirky and irreverent way the brand communicates with its target audience.

There is a supermarket chain in the UK that actively promotes the fact that the milk in its dairy section has been produced from cows that come from within a five kilometre radius of the store. This is a great story that lends itself to authenticity for both the brand of milk and the store in which it is sold. Wouldn't you rather buy locally produced milk from your grocery store?

Another brand with a fantastic story is SPANX shapewear and its founder, Sara Blakely. As the SPANX website tells it, Blakely was 'working as a sales trainer by day and performing stand-up comedy at night, and I didn't know the first thing about the pantyhose industry (except I dreaded wearing pantyhose)'. In 1998 Blakely cut the feet out of her pantyhose to look 'smashing in her cream-coloured pants', and decided that there was a market for footless body-shaping pantyhose. That same year she was awarded the patent for her new product and with a lot of initiative, persistence and hard work she got her business off the ground. With some help from Oprah (who included SPANX pantyhose on her Oprah's Favourite Things list for the year 2000) the brand took off and in 2002 Blakely was named Ernst & Young's Entrepreneur of the Year. It's a wonderful authentic story that has helped promote SPANX to the successful brand it is today.

In chapter 1 I mentioned a company from Perth called Aurenda, which works in injury cost reduction for large corporations. When I first came across Aurenda, I was intrigued by its name and went to its website to find out more about it. It turns out that Aurenda, according to Native Americans, is the unifying spirit that connects mankind to each other, which I thought was wonderful. The story of Aurenda is truly reflected in the values of the brand and the people that work on it.

As someone who has been on a gluten-free diet for almost 15 years it has been fascinating to watch this category explode with brands that are moving in to help solve my problem. For many businesses this expanding category offers a new category into which to extend their product lines. My caution to these companies is that they must ensure that they have a real story. Recently I discovered the following printed on the side of a box of gluten-free bars that I had just bought: 'Established in 1985, this company is dedicated to producing high-quality food products. As a niche manufacturer of snack products, sports bars and speciality confectionary, we concentrate on producing nutritious and delicious-tasting products'. This statement is not a story by any stretch of the imagination; it just tells me what the company does in typically commercial terms. A story gives a brand its emotive authenticity—it's why you started the business, it's what the brand stands for, it's how you give back to the community—all of these things represent the values and essence of the company or brand.

So what's *your* story? Go to your website, company profile or induction manuals and see how well your company's story is articulated. Does your company even have one? In most cases I find that websites say something along the lines of 'We started in 1962 as a customer-focused company that manufactures blah blah blah, jargon jargon jargon'. In this situation there's no emotion, no depth and no real behind-the-scenes understanding of how that company started or what it's about. People desire authenticity. They want to know your story and they want it presented in their language. So work out what your story is, make sure it's authentic, and then communicate it to the world.

Have a strong online presence

As an aside, you may have noticed that I repeatedly make reference to websites. The reason for this is that the first thing people tend to do when they need information on anything is to search for it on the internet. Whether you like it or not, websites are generally our main method of communication

...it's imperative to maintain a quality, up-to-date web presence.

with our target audience, and in today's mobile world it's imperative to maintain a quality, up-to-date web presence. Increasingly, the lives of your target audience are busy and complicated—everyone is juggling home, work, social life and other commitments, and as a consequence business is being done on the run, which is all the more reason for you to have a solid online presence. The online environment has huge potential for communicating with your core customers, and it can also be a tool for them to connect and better understand what you do, via blogs, audio and video podcasts and so on.

Another reason I make mention of the internet so often is that, for me, if your website is not up to date with the changing face of branding, then it's symptomatic of what I can expect to see in an internal and/or external audit of your company and brand. The number of times I hear the comment, 'Our website is in development, don't worry about that, we're getting it redone' is concerning and, as I point out to my clients regularly, your customer doesn't know this. For your customer, right now, right there, he or she is getting a perception of you and your organisation. And trust me, if your website is not right, then the chances are that nothing else in your organisation will carry the correct positioning or authentic story and ultimately will not be enhancing or creating a perception in the mind of your target audience.

It's also worth noting that the internet is becoming one of the main media portals for many advertisers. In the US in 2006 Google and Yahoo! booked more advertising than the CBS, NBC and ABC television networks put together.

Be more than a brand

Another trend having a big impact on brands today is the expectation of customers and clients that you will go above and beyond the mere delivery of your product. Increasingly, your target wants to know what you're doing for the community, the planet and/or charitable organisations—they want you to be more than just a brand. In 2008 the finalists in the Australian Ad News Campaign of the Year were the Climate Institute, Earth Hour and the New South Wales Road and Traffic Authority's 'Pinkie' campaign, all of which were based on areas other than straight corporate communication.

Some companies, such as Method, have even developed a range of environmentally friendly products. From Saab planting native trees on behalf of its customers to offset carbon emissions and Cascade beer promoting its 'green' beer, which is 100 per cent carbon offset, to the GAP stores in the US with their range of Red clothing (with all profits going to support the Red campaign for Africa)—all these companies are focusing on giving back to the community and/or the environment. In fact, shoe designer Kenneth Cole has built his whole brand essence and position around the fight to find a cure for AIDS. If you visit Kenneth Cole's website, you will see some extraordinary visuals of his designs and you can also see who he's banded together with to help fight AIDS. Kenneth Cole believes 'what you stand for means more than what you stand in'.

If you want to encourage more sales, it's important to remember not to make a token effort in giving back to your community; it has to be genuine. For example, an audience member I spoke to at a conference told me about the time she went to a chemist to buy some headache tablets, which cost $8, and noticed that on the box it said that 10 cents from every sale went to charity. She felt that this was not charity, it was merely paying lip service to the idea of giving back. Today's consumer is seeing through organisations that make token attempts to be more than a brand, so beware your intentions.

At the other end of the spectrum, the Savings & Loans credit union that I mentioned in chapter 2 has developed specific measurements for its corporate social responsibility that are reported to the company's shareholders.

It uses a method called the Corporate Responsibility Index (CRI) as a measure of its performance in terms of corporate social responsibility, and it has incorporated its desire for corporate responsibility into the business's culture, showing how serious it is about giving back to the community. Savings & Loans is certainly becoming more than just a brand.

One of the key supporters of the Tour de Cure cycling foundation, of which I am a co-founder, makes a substantial cash donation to the tour each year, but in return requires no exposure, despite the tour now generating millions of dollars worth of awareness and raising substantial revenue in the fight against cancer. This company does it simply because it's the right thing to do, it meets its own articulated measurements of success and, interestingly, the only place the company promotes it is internally to its staff. Remember that I mentioned earlier how stars want to work with stars? Well, new employees of this particular company would certainly be aware of what this company is doing to give back to the community.

...your customers, clients and staff all want to know that the company is committed to giving back.

Whether it's based around community, charitable organisations or sustainability, your customers, clients and staff all want to know that the company is committed to giving back. This is what it means to be more than a brand. If you can't articulate what your brand is doing for the community or the planet, then you're missing an opportunity to build a positive vibe around your brand.

The generous brand

The generous brand is an extension of being more than just a brand. I'll explain this further by using the example of Apple, surely the leader in new-age marketing. Apple ticks all the boxes I've outlined so far in this book to create a positive vibe for its brand. It's also a very generous brand, which adds to the core customer base of raving fans around the world. Anyone who has been to an Apple retail store knows that going there is not just a visit, it's an event. Whenever you visit one of its stores there are almost as many staff members as there are customers, and all the staff are happy to share their knowledge and demonstrate how the many Apple products perform. The stores also have staff members, such as the Mac Genius and Apple trainers, who are there to solve your specific problems or show you how to better use your technology, either on a one-on-one basis or in a group situation, whichever suits you better. What's more, it's all free.

One of the key points we can take from Apple is that its philosophy seems to be 'help me, don't sell me'. As a Mac user I also have the option of receiving weekly quick tips (60-second video podcasts that feature an Apple staff member demonstrating how to better use an Apple product or program). I can also receive updates on everything Apple through the keynote addresses Apple's CEO, Steve Jobs, and other executives, give at worldwide developers' conferences, which are available as podcasts shortly after the event takes place. It's all the things that Apple continually does, all free of charge, that continue to build its global brand.

In August 2009 well-known author Alain de Botton staged an interesting stunt in Terminal 5 at Heathrow Airport in the UK, spending a week in the airport terminal writing a book. Passengers arriving at and departing from the airport formed the characters in the book and were asked to contribute stories and anecdotes for Alain to include. As he wrote, his copy was projected onto a giant screen for passers-by to read. The book was published the following month and 10 000 free copies were given out to passengers. A great stunt perhaps, but it does highlight the move brands are making towards being more generous.

By being a generous brand you're able to build a community of supporters for your brand. Nowadays, there is a sweeping trend away from selling towards helping. Remember, your target audience is a group of people who share a common problem. When you can go above and beyond what your competitors are doing in terms of helping them solve their problems, then you'll increase the loyalty of your target and grow your community. It's not good enough to just provide customers with a product or service—outstanding brands must deliver over and above expectations.

Here are some examples of what other organisations are doing to apply that same generous thinking to their brand:

➧ Head into any Woolworths supermarket and you will see its *Fresh* magazine. During the year shoppers are charged for it, but at Christmas it's free.

➤ Some credit unions offer discounted rates on car loans to people who buy hybrid cars.

➤ In May 2007, 11 Ikea stores across Canada started recognising environmentally conscious customers by providing them with two designated 'green' parking spaces reserved specifically for drivers of hybrid cars and fuel-efficient vehicles. This is becoming more common, with retail stores, hotels, stadiums and university campuses providing such parking spaces.

➤ MINI offers its customers free roadside assistance, free movie tickets, gifts and online support.

➤ In New York since 2007 HSBC has sent a number of branded vintage taxis, vans and even a London cab into Manhattan, and New Yorkers who are able to show the driver an HSBC bank card get a free ride.

➤ ING Direct cafes have popped up in New York, Los Angeles, Philadelphia and Honolulu for the use of its customers. They don't just serve free coffee and snacks; mortgage seminars are also on the menu. ING believes the free seminars will help make the home-buying process a little less complicated for its customers.

➤ Palmeiras, one of the major football teams in Brazil, reserves 5000 seats exclusively for Visa customers. Called the Visa Sector the section has a lounge, bar, restaurants, plasma TVs and other perks. More importantly, it allows the true fans to buy tickets in advance without queuing, using their Visa card.

These are just a few of the many examples from Australia and around the world of companies that truly wish to be viewed as more than just a brand by their target audience. In brand terms it's been called 'perkonomics'. What generous things can you do for your customers or clients? How can you elevate your brand in the eyes of your target?

Loyalty programs

Loyalty programs have long been used by many organisations to reward their customers for their continued loyalty to the brand. I see this type of loyalty program as old marketing, as the problem with these traditional loyalty programs (used in Australia by companies such as Qantas, FlyBuys, Dymocks or Starwood Hotels) is that only those who continue to spend money benefit.

Companies are beginning to think differently about loyalty and it seems that the new approach (what I call the new marketing) is all about building a community. The only way to truly develop a community among your target audience is by over-delivering and establishing a two-way conversation with your client or customer. It's about getting your customers to fall in love with your brand, which goes above and beyond traditional loyalty (which is a decidedly one-sided conversation). By establishing a two-way dialogue with your customers and by helping them rather than

The only way to truly develop a community among your target audience is by over-delivering ...

selling to them, you build loyalty—people will *want* to choose your brand rather than *have* to choose your brand. The aim is to build a community around a shared interest—that is, the product or category that you've created or the problem that you can solve—and then you can communicate the extras that you can provide them with. Again, Apple is a perfect example of this. It is a generous brand that has successfully built a community by constantly delivering the extras and both talking and listening to its target audience.

Nespresso, the coffee-machine concept developed by Nestlé, is another great example of building a community around a brand. Nespresso is successfully building a community based around the shopping experience, its creative execution and the extras it provides in the form of free offers, tips on coffee making and chocolates. From its flagship stores around the world to its classy packaging and outstanding customer service, Nespresso is building a community that many companies would be envious of.

The Nespresso concept is based on the use of the coffee pod, which is inserted into the Nespresso coffee machine to make cafe-style coffee at home. Central to the concept is the necessity of purchasing additional pods, which either keeps you in contact with the stores physically or with its website. Nespresso has actively sought to make the experience of going into the stores to buy the coffee pods part of the attraction that leads to the community. Not only are the colour-coded coffee pods a clever way of customising the taste of the Nespresso coffee to your palette, but the pods themselves are beautifully packaged and presented in long boxes, all of which adds to the premium feel of the brand. Every quarter community members receive premiums in the mail, such as special offers on limited edition espresso cups and chocolates, which are individually packaged in a box delivered to your door. Its television campaign is discrete, classy and uses George Clooney to reinforce its image. Nespresso is successfully growing its community through the unique shopping experience, the creative execution and by delivering over and above its customers' expectations. By offering so much more it is building a brand that people want to own.

True loyalty today is about your customers or clients wanting to be a part of your community. They *show* their loyalty in response to what it is that you provide them— the extras (including audio and video podcasts, blogs, tips, additional information, alliances, free downloads, free gifts, and advance notice of new products, services or launches) make them feel special.

Customisation

Another growing trend in marketing is customisation —that is, tailoring your brand to the needs of your target audience. In contrast to the 'off-the-shelf, one-size-fits-all' mentality of recent times, brands are now looking to personalise what they offer to each target. A good example of this in Australia is Sunsilk, which offers its target 16 different shampoos. No matter what your hair type, there is a specific product for you. Other examples include Ralph Lauren offering to have a Ralph Lauren shirt tailor-made for you, Prescriptives offering tailor-made skincare ranges that are personalised to your individual skin type, Levi's producing made-to-measure jeans and MINI promoting the fact that its cars are customised to each of its buyers. It's said that if you own a MINI you'll never see one on the street that's exactly the same as yours. The UK supermarket example I mentioned earlier promotes the fact that the milk in its dairy section comes from the local area, which means that it has been personalised to the shoppers

...brands are now looking to personalise what they offer to each target.

of that particular store. Kleenex has also run a campaign where photos of its target audience have been printed on its tissue packaging. Nike even ran a campaign in 2007 that showed Ronaldinho, one of the world's greatest soccer players, designing his own sports shoe. He designed the look and feel, chose the colours, and had it made specifically for him.

The online world is also facilitating this trend of custom-isation. From personalised calendars to photo albums and stationery, the options are becoming almost limitless. These days you can even customise books and have your child's name embedded into the story as the main character of a book.

This trend towards customisation is at the forefront of most progressive companies. There's no doubt that custom-isation is here to stay and, if anything, it's only going to become more prevalent. As a marketer you need to work out how you can customise your product, business or service to your target audience.

Media has changed

Not only have branding and marketing changed, but so too has media consumption. Once upon a time marketers had limited media options and often also budgetary constraints, whereas today there are countless options for marketers to choose from, and a significant number of those options can be done for nothing or at low cost. For example, anyone can post a video on YouTube at no cost and it can be viewed by millions of people within a week. The changes in new media are very powerful and demand that we think differently about how we approach the use of media.

These days the smart people skip ads. We're too busy, we've got too much information coming at us, we're time poor, we're all on fast-forward and what's more we're increasingly being selfish with our attention. We fast-forward through ads, we flick through magazines, we Google at the speed of light and we multi-task while we do it. This means that, as a brand, you have to be even more diligent in getting your message across. You must have the fundamentals correct, you must be succinct in your delivery and you must be able to communicate in a language that helps people and doesn't sell to them. There is no time for a learning curve, but the new media front doesn't have to be that scary if you just take the time to watch, listen, learn and think about how you can make it appropriate to your target audience. Don't try to copy everyone else, because their way of doing things and their message will not necessarily be appropriate for your target audience. It needs to be personalised to the issues and problems facing your target audience in a manner that suits them.

Here are some figures about the impact of the internet and the ways in which media has changed and is changing. In 2008 internet advertising spending in the UK was greater than the amount spent on radio, outdoor and magazine advertising. In that same year in any given month 79 per cent of people interviewed had used search engines, and according to marketing information service WARC in 2008 one-third of the television consumption in the United States was online. Once upon a time you had to have a physical retail outlet, whereas today people can shop online 24/7. Once upon a time you swamped people with spam, but today you need permission to contact them. Subscriptions, RSS feeds, blogs, Twitter, LinkedIn—all ask permission for you and your brand to communicate with your customers.

These changes also raise serious considerations for companies and brands of all sizes, some of which are adapting better and more quickly than others. The watchmaker Longines came up with the novel idea of running an SC:09 ski challenge online, which was a game of skill based around skiing. It was an interesting way to promote itself by embedding its brand into a free online game, and then distributing it to the world. As another example, Wrangler jeans installed a free Wrangler

Laundromat at the Glastonbury music festival. A bit closer to home, Tooheys has run its Tooheys Uncharted promotion, which provides an avenue of potential discovery for unsigned cover bands. Pedigree dog food's website <www.puppy.com.au> lists puppy-friendly parks and paths in Australia. A lot of these brands are not only being generous and delivering more than just a brand, they are also embedding their brand into user-friendly websites, games or environments that don't just try to sell their products, but also help the consumer. They entertain, inform and solve problems.

You must be constantly putting yourself in the shoes of your target audience...

As an aside, the Ronaldinho commercial to promote the Nike shoes was run primarily on the Nike website as a video podcast. Television commercials are now being produced specifically for the web and often may never see the light of day on traditional television. This opens up a whole new avenue of promotion for a lot of companies that, up until now, was thought to be out of reach because of cost constraints.

The question for your own brand is what can you do to take advantage of these changes to the media landscape, as well as being generous and going above and beyond as a brand? Don't place a ceiling over your thinking by saying it doesn't apply to you, that you work in the trucking industry and your clients don't care about any of that. Don't assume that truck drivers are immune to new media and don't think that housewives are immune to mobile phones, email or iPods. They all use it, and if you're not taking advantage of these trends, your competitor may be and if that's the case, you'll be left behind. Remember, don't just use the change in the media landscape to blow your whistle and try to sell more. Use it to *help* your target. Use blogs, vidcasts, podcasts, web forums, Facebook, MySpace, Twitter and the like, and make sure you use them effectively to help problem-solve. You must be constantly putting yourself in the shoes of your target audience and trying to think as they would. They are asking themselves, how are you going to help me? I don't care about you. I care about me and what you can do for me.

Some banks are now having more interaction with their customers via Twitter than they are via traditional telephone communication. In 140 characters, customers are able to register complaints, ask questions or seek clarity on issues. I have heard of banks setting up actual customer service departments based on the Twitter application in order to serve their customers quickly, more efficiently and by the means that better suits their customers. Brands such as Whole Foods Market, a supermarket selling the highest quality natural and organic foods in the UK and the US, even have iPhone applications allowing you, at the flick of a thumb, access to recipes, product information, locations and ingredients all from its supermarket. The chain also has almost 100 000 people following it on Twitter, interacting with it daily on specials, new products, new information and health advice. Whole Foods Market really has adopted the new media space well and has made it work in a way that is relevant to its target audience.

Sam Walton from Walmart was famous for saying, 'High expectations are the key to everything'. Set the expectations for your brand at the highest possible level. Take advantage of these emerging trends by breaking free from traditional thinking and old paradigms, and step out and do something bold and adventurous that will separate you from everyone else in your market.

Promoting to the five senses

One marketing trend that I find fascinating is sensory marketing. In his book *Brand Sense* Martin Lindstrom talks about the importance of stimulating the senses in order to hit as many different touch points as possible with your brand. He gives many examples of companies overseas that are working their consumers through touch points related to the five senses—touch, taste, smell, sight and sound.

Following are some examples of the way each sense has been successfully used by some brands that I hope will help stimulate your own thinking and encourage you to apply this thinking to elevate your own brand.

Sight

About 45 to 55 per cent of all people learn primarily through sight via the use of colour, graphs, icons and pictures. A great example of a visually distinct brand is

Tiffany & Co. For most women the Tiffany & Co. blue box is a highly anticipated part of the buying experience. Brands such as Tiffany & Co., David Jones and MINI, and service stations such as BP and Shell, have invested a great deal of time and money to create a brand that is easily recognisable.

I'm amazed at the high percentage of websites that use lots of words rather than a few simple pictures to communicate their message. I recall meeting with a manufacturing company that specialises in forging steel. It has an excellent website, which features beautiful large colour photos of its steel furnaces in action — flames,

How well do your marketing materials and website use the power of sight?

sparks and all the glowing colours of flames as steel is forged are shown. The company's CEO proudly told me that a German manufacturer had chosen the company's product based purely on its website and, as a result, his company had just doubled the turnover of its business. How well do your marketing materials and website use the power of sight?

Sound

The 'zoom zoom' ad campaign developed by Mazda is a great example of what is called a sound mnemonic. If you were to hear nothing else in a Mazda commercial except the 'zoom zoom' sound, you would instantly know which car manufacturer the ad was for. Likewise, the sound of a Harley Davidson motorbike driving down the street is unmistakable. One of the most successful examples of the sound mnemonic is the three-second Intel jingle that runs as part of any computer program that carries the Intel Centrino processor. That little sound and nothing else tells you that the computer carries an Intel chip. It's a clever tool, but again, it only resonates because the company uses it over and over and over again.

Qantas has done a wonderful job of using sound in its branding with the use of Peter Allen's song 'I Still Call Australia Home'. Whether you hear the song played in a television commercial or on an in-flight audio track, it evokes all sorts of patriotic emotions. The company also uses it strategically at major events, such as the AFL Grand Final, the World Cup, the Olympics and the Bledisloe Cup, or at times when we think of family such as at Christmas. This combination of sight and sound has been particularly successful for the brand.

Another successful Australian example is the sound mnemonic that Schweppes has created, which is known as 'Schweppervescence'. Schweppes uses this mnemonic on its website, and on its television and radio ads.

If you are an accounting firm, a law firm or a flower distribution company, using sound to make your company recognisable may not be something that immediately springs to mind. Yet, wouldn't it be interesting to work out how you might be able to create a mnemonic sound that relates back to your brand. It's so easy to do, yet most people don't think to do it.

Touch

Touch as a form of sensory marketing can range from the furnishings in your workplace, to your stationery and the quality of the paper used in the presentations you give to your clients, to the way your product is packaged and presented.

In 2008 HSBC and ad agency JWT Sydney launched a campaign to teach the bank's customers how to make origami out of their ATM receipts. All ATM receipts featured instructions on the back that showed customers how to fold them into an array of different shapes. The shapes represented and reinforced the personal banking solutions available to HSBC customers. For example, one set of instructions showed how to create a house, which promoted HSBC home loans. This is a pretty cool concept that any number of banks could have taken advantage of, but no-one else saw it. It's simple, it's original, it engages the senses in more ways than one and it's effective. And let's face it, origami that also advertises home loans is a whole lot more interesting than picking up a leaflet on the subject in the branch!

The Apple iPod, Nano, iTouch and iPhone are also excellent examples of a multi-sensory experience using touch, sight and sound. They feel great, look spectacular and have great functionality. Apple has capitalised on this by devoting an area of its retail stores to allowing existing and potential customers to experience the tactile nature of its products. In fact, it has been a huge selling point that has set the company apart from any other music or telecommunications company in the market.

Taste

Taste as a form of marketing is challenging for most brands. When Coca-Cola changed the formula, and hence the taste, of its product in 1985 it became one of the great case studies in marketing and brand history because customers deserted the brand in droves. Coca-Cola was forced to reintroduce the original formula and brand it as Coca-Cola Classic. One wonders whether the public reaction was based on the new taste or whether it was the perception of someone tampering with a well-known brand that was the issue. Perception can be a powerful thing.

... with a little imagination any brand can use any one of the senses...

One company that uses sight, touch and taste is Toblerone. It has been clever in delivering not only a great taste, but also a unique shape that differentiates it from any other chocolate. It's the tactile nature of Toblerone when you break the bar that appeals to the senses.

When I spoke to a group of CEOs about sensory marketing, one person related the following story. His wife had gone to collect their car from a BMW dealership, as it had been serviced. On arrival she was told the car was not quite ready, and she was then invited to enjoy an espresso coffee and chocolates while she waited for the car. When her husband asked how much the service had cost, she responded, 'I don't know, but the chocolates and coffee were delicious'. It just goes to show that with a little imagination any brand can use any one of the senses if they put their minds to it. Do you think the experience would have been the same if BMW had served instant coffee in an old mug with stale biscuits? Turn something ordinary into something exceptional.

Smell

I bet everyone can remember the smell of Play Dough, and it's a good example of how smell can be used to identify a brand. Smell is probably one of the hardest senses for most traditional organisations to get their head around. Naturally it's easy for anyone who's working in perfumes, food, wine, gardens or internal furnishings, but it's a lot harder for traditional services or the manufacturing or industrial areas. However, if you challenge yourself, who knows what you may come up with. Don't simply write it off as something that will never work in your industry, because chances are that a competitor will make the effort and then use it against you.

The Executive Connection (TEC) is the world's leading CEO organisation, bringing member CEOs together on a monthly basis to give them the opportunity to learn and develop their leadership skills. I recently spoke to a TEC group on the topic of sensory marketing and one of the members who was the CEO of an aged-care facility commented that as a company they had worked very hard to alleviate the 'old person's home' smell that was evident when visiting older style aged-care facilities, as they had found it had a negative impact on their potential residents. The facility was in the process of making changes to ensure that the sensory experience was new and refreshing, and in complete contrast to perhaps what people were expecting.

The multi-sensory experience

The more senses you are able to engage for your product or service, the more successful you will be. The interesting thing about sensory marketing is that sometimes you can work with just one sense and sometimes you can use more than one. The head of Roland Keyboards told me that once upon a time when marketing keyboards, it used to be all about how they sounded, but today it's not only about how they sound, but also about how they feel, and, more to the point, how they look. Roland has had to change its whole approach and expand its appeal to senses other than sound. Who could have guessed that today keyboards need to look great, feel great and sound outstanding!

In the airline industry Singapore Airlines has long placed considerable emphasis on sensory marketing with its Singapore Girl campaign. The airline is very stringent with regards to all the sensory modalities, particularly for their flight attendants who must look and sound the part. According to branding expert Martin Lindstrom, the women the airline employs are required to be under the age of 26 and not outgrow their tailor-made uniform.

Its food and other aspects of its in-flight service also must comply with certain sensory parameters.

Given that 70 per cent of decisions are made in the last four seconds of purchase in store, the power of packaging has never been greater. In fact, there are many agencies and companies now that specialise in packaging. A product needs to look outstanding, feel great and, in some cases, even smell and taste right in order to stimulate the shopper.

Look at your own product and apply the senses and see how many you hit. If you work in the service industry, then your packaging is not only the product you send out, it's also your documentation and the freebies you give to clients to help sell your message. A lot of organisations put in only an average amount of effort to stimulate the senses of their target audience. Their company literature, website and general presentation leave a lot to be desired. They fail to see sensory marketing as an outstanding opportunity to position themselves and set a certain standard for their brand.

> *A product needs to look outstanding, feel great and, in some cases, even smell and taste right...*

In researching a building group I was about to do some work with, I made a point of visiting its website. I found that it didn't have a clear target or position and gave me no indication of why the company was different from any other building group. I wasn't even sure what area it specialised in. When I challenged the CEO about the poor website, his response was that the company didn't get many visitors to its website, that it was just for architects and even then, mainly just to give out information. I then asked him what he would need to do to make his website a vital resource for any architect. He said, 'I guess it comes from providing information, new trends and advice', which was a great answer, because in doing so he would be engaging a number of the senses that had been ignored on the website. Visually he could use photographs or video of new buildings, and unique and award-winning architectural designs. By adding podcasts he would be engaging the sense of sound and by creating a 'feel' for the website he could perhaps even engage the tactile nature of his target.

The challenge for all marketers is to be aware of the five senses and learn how to make use of as many as possible in the marketing of your brand. The building group could quite easily incorporate taste and smell into its brand messaging, through educational events with wine, beer, food and maybe chocolates. Real estate agents continue to sell a lot of houses by ensuring there is coffee brewing or fresh flowers in the house during inspection times. This is an extreme example, but I'm just trying to stimulate ideas in your own mind that you can apply to your brand.

Listen to your target audience

In my work with the University of South Australia I have had the pleasure of talking with earth scientist Professor Martin Williams about business strategy and research. He mentioned that the word research comes from the French word *rechercher*, which means 'to look again', which I thought was fascinating, as I believe that today a lot of marketers are relying on research to tell them what to do. In truth, research can't tell you what to do, it can only give you a chance to 'look again' and inform you about how you and/or your competitors are perceived in the marketplace. Research will tell you what worked, what didn't work and, if done properly, it can also give you an understanding of whether the battle for the mind of your target audience is succeeding or failing. This in itself is valuable, but I don't suggest that you use research to tell you what you *should* be doing. Nothing replaces your own market research or listening to your target audience.

One of the biggest traditional retailers in the world is Walmart. In Sam Walton's book *Sam Walton: Made in America* he mentions habitually walking up and down the aisles of his stores, talking to customers to find out what value he could bring to their life. He would question shoppers with a pair of socks and ask if they were great value. If yes, that was great, if not, what do I need to do? I worked for Westfield Shopping Centres with Frank Lowy and John Saunders for many years. John would fly from Sydney to my shopping centre in Brisbane and arrange to meet me at the centre at 11 am. Invariably it would be 11.45 am or later when John would arrive. I'd ask him whether the flight was delayed and he would reply that he was in the back of the taxi having a delightful discussion so he told the driver to keep driving. John would drive around the suburbs of Brisbane chatting to taxi drivers, as he knew that taxi drivers had an opinion on everything and they would give it to him straight. He would ask them about his shopping centre car parks, his department stores, the delicatessen or what people thought of his school holiday entertainment. That's where John did his research and he's one of the smartest entrepreneurs that I've met. When John arrived at the shopping centre, the first thing he would do was walk around, observe, talk to and ask questions of his staff, the retailers and the shoppers. He was always asking questions in order to find and discover. This was his personal research.

I always recommend people undertake a listening tour...

Every brand manager should take a leaf out of John and Sam's book. I always recommend people undertake a listening tour—that is, going on the road and listening to your target audience. Your target audience is a group of people who share a common problem, and your job is to get out of your office, walk among those people and find out what those problems are. Don't imagine what they are, don't surmise what they are and certainly don't assume you know what's really going on unless you are walking among those people.

In chapter 1 I mentioned coming across a young strategist, Jeremy, who had asked very pertinent questions during a session at a brewery. The session was on a Monday, so during the course of conversation I asked Jeremy what he had done on the weekend. It turned out that he had been to one of the big music festivals in Sydney, not necessarily to see the bands, but more to 'Just walk around and see what's going on. See who's wearing what, who's doing what, what people are saying, what they're drinking and how they're doing it'. This is true research.

I relayed this story to another group at a later time and in the audience happened to be someone who had worked in the alcohol industry for many years. As I made the previous point he started laughing, raised his hand and said, 'You know, I worked for one of Australia's big brewers and my day was eight hours of meetings, and then I started checking emails. You're exactly right, we lose touch with the drinker'. Have you lost touch with your target audience? As Mark Twain once said, 'A man who carries a cat by the tail learns something he can learn in no other way'.

I've been known to do my own market research in preparation for my speeches. On one particular occasion I was in a taxi on my way to present to a group of credit unions, and I asked the taxi driver what he knew about credit unions, to get a person-on-the-street's view of the industry. He said, 'I'm not really sure, but I think...' and off he went. We chatted for 20 minutes about his perceptions of credit unions, which ended up being the basis for my speech. What he had articulated was spot on. Now, I'm not suggesting you should drive around in the back of taxis to do all your research, but you do need to work out where your target audience are and what can be done to work out how they feel, what they do, what they're thinking and how they perceive you and/or your competitors. Traditional marketing is asking questions, listening, thinking and then making the next move. If you're serious about elevating your brand to outstanding, you'll have to step outside your comfort zone. The best way to do this is by researching and walking among your target audience.

I'll finish this section with a great quote that I read, from the CEO of UK department store Marks & Spencer, Stuart Rose. He had left the company after 17 years to work on another venture. Following his departure M&S started to slip as a brand and its sales were reflecting that. After some time Rose went back to the business because he believed he knew what had to be done. His diagnosis of what had gone wrong in the business can be summed up by the following:

> If it looks like a duck and quacks like a duck, then it's a duck, right? That's how I operate. I'm not going to take the duck's bloody footprints, send them away for DNA analysis and find 10 weeks later that it's a duck, by which time it's flown away. That's where I think [M&S] have been a bit slow here sometimes. It's analysis-paralysis.

Rose has since turned the business around and put M&S back on the road to regaining the positive perception that it had held for many years.

It's not about you knowing your customer, it's about your customer knowing you. Even seven-time Tour de France champion cyclist Lance Armstrong did research on his competitors. As he said, 'You can know your opponent and that gets you into the vault, but it doesn't get you the money. You have to do the work'.

Elevate your brand above others in your category by thinking creatively about how to spend your money and reap the rewards. Remember, don't make token gestures, you need to do it properly. Sometimes it's better to invest in these areas rather than just produce the standard brochure, flyer or corporate profile that everybody else does, just because everybody else does it.

Vibe status

⏵ Are you keeping an eye on the current trends? If yes, is your brand taking advantage of these trends?

⏵ Does your brand have an authentic story?

⏵ Is your brand generous?

⏵ Are you tailoring your brand to the needs of your target audience?

⏵ Are you taking advantage of new media?

⏵ Are you using sensory marketing?

⏵ Are you conducting market research? Are you listening to your target audience?

Chapter 4

The eight cylinders of marketing

This chapter sets out the top eight tips, tools and observations that I've gathered from working with many successful organisations around the world. When applied to your brand, these tips, tools and observations may be all it takes to give it a little extra punch and enable it to become world class.

Brand performance is similar to the performance of a car—for it to be working to its full potential the car has to be using all its cylinders. Too often, however, organisations that I work with are working on anything *but* all eight cylinders. They may be doing some things well and others not so well, or they may have great potential, but whatever their situation, often all they need are a few extra cylinders to really give their brand some punch. I've found the following eight cylinders to be the ones that are most likely to make the biggest difference to your brand.

Cylinder 1: public relations

Public relations (PR) is a very underused tool in organisations of all sizes. I've been fortunate to work with some brilliant PR companies, both on my own brand and also when working with other companies. Used well, PR is a brilliant way to help build your brand. It's been said you should use PR to build the brand and advertising, and promotion to maintain it. However, a lot of organisations tend to waste their time, energy and money by not using their PR effectively.

I spoke to some of the best people I know in the PR industry (from small boutique agencies to large multinationals) and asked them for their key pieces of advice when using PR, which I've consolidated into three points:

➤ have a newsworthy story about your brand

➤ put together a brief about your brand

➤ integrate your marketing and public relations.

Let's take a look at each element in detail.

Have a newsworthy story about your brand

With changes in the media landscape, it's more difficult to get PR coverage today than ever before. The pressure for ratings and readership, over-commercialisation and the quality of stories that are presented have meant that news reports, magazines, trade journals and even some blogs are being increasingly selective about what they run.

As I learned when I first started using PR, what *I* might think is newsworthy is not necessarily newsworthy in the eyes of an editor. As a result, I would suggest sitting with your PR consultant for a couple of hours each month to work up a story about your brand. In my case, I would go through my material and discuss with the consultant my philosophies, angles, ideas for stories, things I'd written or may have heard, and I would leave it to my consultant to find what she saw as being the stories within my stories. I was often frustrated, believing I had a really newsworthy story, when in actual fact I didn't. The important lesson I learned was that for PR to work, it's all about the story — not the story in your mind, but the story in the mind of an editor or publisher. The best and easiest way to understand what is newsworthy is to let your publicist guide you to the correct story.

> *...for PR to work, it's all about the story...*

I regularly meet CEOs and managers who tell me they do their own PR. In reality what this generally means is that the CEO or manager writes up what he or she thinks is a newsworthy article or press release, and then sends it out to the media. That's not true PR. True PR is using a consultant who can recognise a real story, write a press release, and then position it so that the media picks it up. A consultant also has the time to follow up with journalists, suggest interesting angles and potentially get you the valuable media space that you are after. PR is most valuable and advantageous when you have some-one else talking about you and building a positive vibe for your brand in the media for free. But once again, it all comes down to having the right story in the first place. Some may argue that PR is expensive compared with the cost of producing magazines, newspapers, brochures, profiles or catalogues, but it's a great investment if it's used well.

Put together a brief about your brand

The next essential piece of the PR puzzle is the brief about your brand. This is one of the most important pieces, not just in terms of getting you exposure, but also in terms of building both your brand and a positive vibe around your company. The first thing you should do with any consultant is run through your marketing model with them. It's important to reiterate the audience you are aiming at, what you are about, your positioning, your category, the word you want to own and what you have done to promote your brand since you last touched base. By continually going back to the brief your PR consultant will be clear on the outcomes you want to achieve.

I consider myself to be a minnow in an ocean of brands, yet I've had stories placed in some of the biggest newspapers in Australia and have actually had my positioning quoted in the first paragraph of some articles—for example, 'Gary Bertwistle helps companies unlock their great ideas'. This is media gold! It just goes to show how valuable PR can be to any organisation, particularly the smaller brands with limited resources. And whenever you meet with your consultant, revisit your marketing model before you start developing new stories.

Integrate your marketing and public relations

Quite often PR and/or the PR department is viewed as separate from the marketing department, and in some organisations, public relations staff are seen as the ones who deal with the disputes and problems as opposed to being a core part of a brand council. Your consultant and/or PR team should be an integral part of the council setting the strategy for your brand. If it's an external consultant, involve him or her in what you're doing on a regular basis, because unless you're a trained expert who has worked in PR for many years, chances are you don't have the skills to be working in this area of the business.

PR should be integrated into the overall strategy. If you're running a trade magazine campaign, then integrate PR into that. For example, if you're running a full-page advertisement in a trade magazine, then go to the magazine with a newsworthy story that can be run as an editorial piece. Quite often running an ad will give you leverage with the magazine to include a story for free. Once again, you need to go back to your marketing model to ensure that you find a newsworthy story that suits your target and positions you in the right way. As an example, if you are an agricultural distributor of water pumps, you may find it beneficial to run an ad in an agricultural small farming magazine. It could also be an opportunity to run a story on how you run irrigation and water pumps on uneven ground in order to maximise crop potential and paddock yield.

If you're doing a street event, a trade show or an expo, then integrate your PR into that. For example, in addition to running your own trade show display, you could produce a flyer to give to passers-by that outlines the origins and advantages of your product, and your story. This story could then run in the trade show program as an extra feature or insert. The same story could also be used as leverage in your industry's trade magazine to promote not only your stand at the trade show, but also the stories, origins or technology behind your products.

Make a conscious decision to use PR on an ongoing basis...

Make a conscious decision to use PR on an ongoing basis as one of the weapons in your artillery. Unless there is shared meaning in terms of the strategic direction (your marketing model), what you expect and how you measure it, you can't expect the consultant to execute your PR in the manner you want.

Quite often the PR strategy once set is then forgotten. It is important to review your PR regularly. This way you're always on your consultant's radar, and you can remind him or her of your brief and the outcomes you expect (such as column centimetres, television exposure or selling your position), as well being kept updated on where the consultant is at and the calls he or she has made. It may not be something that you want or can do weekly, but I'd certainly suggest no less than fortnightly. PR is a cost-efficient, powerful tool that can create a great vibe around your brand, and if used correctly, won't waste your time, cash or energy.

Cylinder 2: measuring success

How do you know your marketing works? When I pose this question to audiences I get answers such as 'There's an increase in sales', 'We measured the hits to our website', 'More people come through the doors', 'Our volumes go up', 'Our sales reps hear people talking about it' or 'I'm not really sure, it's a bit of a problem'.

Knowing how well, or even if, your marketing is working is one of the great mysteries of marketing. Sales or volume are certainly indicators, as is traffic flow. You could even spend money on a perceptual research study to find out whether you have moved people from one perception to another. All of these are valid indicators of the success or failure of your advertising, but it's important to recognise that they're all implemented *after* the fact. They all measure how well a campaign went after the campaign or promotion has already run. But is it possible to tell *before* you actually run an ad how well it will go?

In his book *Jump Start Your Business Brain,* Doug Hall spoke of a three-step process that he has used in the US to give marketers more confidence about the success of what they're planning to do. He analysed hundreds of campaigns and came up with a formula that he believes can be used by businesses in any category to give them a better chance of succeeding, whether it's via the internet, press ads, flyers or presentations. Here are Hall's three steps, which are well worth using:

1 *Point of difference.* Review your promotional materials and ask yourself whether they show a true point of difference. Do they clearly explain how you are different from your competitors? It's a simple thing that can make a huge difference, but it's regularly overlooked. So often we're too busy telling people what we do and what our product is rather than explaining why it's different. And if you're not clearly articulating why you're different, then you're missing a valuable opportunity. Perception is about joining the dots for people, and if you don't do it for them, they'll do it for themselves, and as a result, they may not be drawing the perception that you would like them to. In this world of mass communication, short attention spans and information overload, you need to identify clearly your point of difference in all of your materials.

2 *Overt benefit.* Does your marketing material demonstrate an overt benefit to your target?

The new generation of client or customer is 'allaboutme.com'—that is, they're only concerned about what's in it for them. Rather than subtly demonstrating the benefit, any benefit must be overt. Your customers and clients are being bombarded by thousands of messages every day via emails, podcasts, blogs, bus shelters, radio commercials, television spots, magazines, newspapers, planes writing messages in the sky, the insides of buses, train stations, foyers and even the bottom of coffee cups. Therefore *all* of your materials must demonstrate the overt benefit of using your product over someone else's.

3   *Give me a reason to believe.* Many marketers can demonstrate a point of difference. A large proportion can even promote an overt benefit. But do you give your target a reason to believe? In an ever-changing economic climate, and with ever-increasing competition in the marketplace, customers and clients need a reason to believe in your product or service. They're asking, 'Why should I trust you, why should I believe you and why should I invest my time and money in your product?' Today more than ever before, people are seeking authenticity, whether that authenticity comes from fact sheets, testimonials or validated research.

To give you an example of a great reason to believe, I worked with a company that manufactures floor tiles. Stoneworld was a terrific company experiencing challenging times and was having a hard time differentiating itself from its competitors. The company, up until that point, used to have a five-year guarantee on their tiles. The CEO stood up during the session and said 'We will now put a 10-year quality assurance on all our products'. He personally wrote to all the clients, suppliers and staff outlining what quality assurance meant and what Stoneworld's new guarantee was. This was double the guarantee that any other retailer was providing. He also developed a 10-year quality assurance certificate, which he gave away to every customer. The company developed a positioning statement, which was 'Stoneworld—Quality Assured'.

Your reason to believe can come from testimonials, how many years you've been in the business, a guarantee, and the representation of your work through photos, stories and reports. It can come from media, stories written about you or something that the breweries call the bar-room defence. When you're trying a new beer you will develop bar-room defence to justify to your friends why you're choosing to drink a different beer. The rationale behind your selection will be clearly articulated so that you can then convince your friends you've made the right choice. Every brand should have this reason to believe, a bar-room defence, to give consumers a reason to believe that what you're saying in your promotion and marketing materials is true.

These three steps can and should be used as a checklist to review potential marketing material before any time, energy or money is spent on its execution. Ideally, your material would demonstrate all three points, giving it the best chance of hitting your target. In most cases, however, you'll find you probably hit two out of three, and that's fine.

So, to establish whether your advertising is going to work, always revisit your marketing model to decide whether this is the right promotional tool to enhance the perception of your product or service in the mind of your target, and then go to the three steps: Is there a demonstrated point of difference? Is there an overt benefit? Does it give customers a reason to believe?

Cylinder 3: tone

Whenever you see or hear a Qantas advertisement you know which airline it's for without ever having to see the logo. Similarly, you don't actually need to see a Kleenex tissue logo, a Calvin Klein logo or an Absolut vodka logo in any of these companies' advertising campaigns, to know which brand they are advertising. The reason is that each of these brands has successfully created a certain tone, personality and feel about everything they do from a marketing standpoint. I'm a great believer that tone can be achieved either through visuals or sound, or maybe even both.

It's said that a picture can say a thousand words and the same is true for any visuals you may use for your brand.

When you conduct your internal and external brand audit and lay all your materials out on the table, examine them to see if there's a uniform tone running through them. From the pictures you choose, to the layout, the font and the colours, all your materials should create a tone or feel for your brand, and this tone should be reproduced in your television and print ads, on your website, in flyers, in brochures and even in packaging. It's about setting a world-class standard for what you're doing through visuals, copy and layout, and then being studious in its application. Excellence is not a singular act but a habit. You are what you repeatedly do.

...all your materials should create a tone or feel for your brand...

Once again Apple is a great example. The store layout, packaging, product design, staff uniforms, website, blogs, and audio and video podcasts all carry the unmistakable Apple design, style and tone. It all feels, looks and sounds distinctly Apple.

All the visuals that you use should bring to life the perception that you want to own in the mind of your target audience. Develop a look and feel for your brand and treat it like it's the world's best. There's a saying in personal development that you should act the way you want to become until you become the way you act. Create a world-class tone, feel and look for all your materials, and before you know it you will have companies all around the world looking at you as a benchmark for your category.

Be honest. Look at your materials and see whether you are truly creating a great vibe through your tone. In fact, when you look at your current materials, what vibe are you creating... if any?

Cylinder 4: elephants dance with elephants

To elevate your brand to the perception you wish to occupy in the mind of your target audience, you need to associate with the right people. You can tell the quality of a brand by the company it keeps—elephants dance with elephants. Often alliances or associations with other brands or individuals can either help or hinder the brand. It all depends on who you associate with. Look at the elephants you currently dance with and ask yourself if they are the right companies, brands or high-profile personalities to be seen with. Do they elevate you and improve the perception of your brand? By association, does it make your brand stretch upwards? By associating yourself with these other brands does it give yours the right vibe?

The people you associate with, the look, the feel, who talks about you, what they say and why they should buy from you are all factors that affect the vibe. For example, if you were to look at a company profile and its client list was made up of high-profile companies that you recognised, you wouldn't need to hear much more of its story to know who that elephant was dancing with. It certainly elevates the brand and gives you a very quick reason to believe.

Ultraceuticals is regarded as a premium Australian skincare brand developed to international quality standards, so I was not surprised when I found its products given to Qantas business class passengers. By simply placing itself in the right spot at the right time Ultraceuticals has been elevated to exactly the place it wants to be perceptually.

In 2005 when Armani opened a store in Collins Street in Melbourne it had a grand opening. Naturally it was attended by the who's who of the fashion industry and it was full of celebrities. They were served Moet & Chandon champagne, San Pelligrino water and Lavazza coffee. Lavazza is sold in supermarkets, but it was elevated in status as a premium Italian coffee brand by being served at that party and associated with luxury brands. What a great piece of branding!

...have contact with your target audience at least every 90 days.

Molton Brown is a UK company producing innovative bath and body, skincare and men's grooming products, home and travel accessories and gift solutions. It does very little, if any, traditional marketing, but gets its perception and profile by dancing with only the best elephants. Molton Brown is always found in all the best hotels, restaurants and first-class airline lounges throughout the world.

So make a list — who do you dance with?

Cylinder 5: the 90-day rule

According to the *Guinness Book of World Records*, the world's greatest car salesman is Carl Sewell. In his book *Customers for Life* Sewell talks about what he calls the 90-day rule. He believes that contact must be made with clients every 90 days to be kept top of mind. Sewell also believes that when he sells a car, he's actually selling 10 or 12 cars. Why? Because if he does an outstanding job of selling to you, you may buy a car for your wife and one for your child, and then recommend him to a friend, who will recommend him to others.

The lesson in Sewell's book is that after 90 days you risk being forgotten. When you are putting together your brand plans, you should plan to have contact with your target audience at least every 90 days. How you do this can be a combination of all of the traditional and non-traditional methods discussed so far in this book. It's also worth considering an element of non-sales-related contact, of which I am a big believer. By non-sales-related contact I mean contact that demonstrates you being more than a brand, and talking to your target as though they are part of your community, with a view to being able to help them, not sell to them.

Many marketers have brand plans that stretch 12 months into the future and although I agree that it's important to plan ahead, a tight 90-day plan is still essential. A 90- to 180-day plan also allows you the flexibility to adjust and adapt to changes in the economy, markets and the minds of customers. Carl von Clausewitz, the Prussian military thinker whose principles have had a strong influence in marketing warfare, believes that war is inherently unpredictable, messy and non-linear. Even Napoleon said, 'War is shrouded in fog'. Consequently, we must be flexible.

When you contact your target be a bit unpredictable. Use a variety of contact points from postcards to personal letters, email, podcasts, sales calls, roadshows, premium giveaways, telephone calls or brochures. Every 90 days choose a different method of contact so as not to become predictable. Many marketers roll out the same plan year after year, just changing the year at the top of the page. You must think differently about how you implement your marketing strategy.

Cylinder 6: jargon

Often when I receive corporate profiles from companies I am about to work with, it seems that whoever wrote the profile chose every advertising, marketing, branding and communication cliché and put them together into a series of pages to try to make an impression. When I question the company's marketers about it, they reply that it's what brand and marketing managers expect to see in a presentation.

The problem I have with this is that people won't read marketing jargon. They look at the creative execution and then go straight to the back page to see how much it's going to cost. Go to your own website and have a good look. People write what they think they *should* write on a website, rather than actually communicating with their target audience on a more personal level. Your website and company profile should be written in terminology that is friendly,

The problem ... is that people won't read marketing jargon.

warm, emotive and tells a story. Forget the jargon and talk to me through your company literature as though I'm sitting in front of you having a conversation.

Websites should be considered a living document. A company profile should be a document that will help build the personality and character of your brand, rather than just a collection of words telling me how long you've been around and what you do. Putting a filter on the jargon will cut through the clutter and help create a better vibe for your brand.

Cylinder 7: velcro

Part of the external audit of your brand should include mapping out all of the potential contact points that sell your message to your target audience. From your business cards, letterhead, invoicing, company profile, brochures, flyers and free gifts to the telephone calls you make, these touch points are all opportunities to sell your vibe. I recently heard it likened to a piece of velcro, the aim being to get as many touch points on the left-hand side of the velcro to touch with those on the right-hand side.

One of the rules of marketing strategy that comes from Sun Tzu in his book *The Art of War* is to use all available resources. That is, map out and line up all of your touch points *before* going to battle with a competitor. While it's easy to quickly put out ad hoc marketing, it's not as effective as getting all available resources lined up. For example, if you have a product launch, it's easy to create a new brochure for the product without considering how it fits in with your overall positioning. Is the same information on your website? Do your sales teams have a true understanding of what's happening? Has the factory or production team been briefed on what's required and why? Has the PR team been advised and has it been discussed with your brand council?

The problem lies when you're too busy with the *doing* to step back and fully map out the touch points. This applies as much to one-off operators as it does to large corporations. When you are so busy multi-tasking, it's easy to forget the basics. You may have updated your letterhead and business cards, but forgotten to include the new copy in your company profile, website or PowerPoint presentations. It needs to become a core part of your vocabulary and an essential ingredient of the DNA of your organisation. Use all available resources to get the necessary traction for your message and positioning with your target audience. Most of us don't have the money to put together big campaigns, which means that we have to rely on every possible contact with our target audience to sell our message. Once again, it's not a money thing, it's a thinking thing. It's taking the time to sit back and map, just like a piece of velcro, all the touch points you have with your customer or client. A true velcro grip only comes when all the touch points are met.

Cylinder 8: strategy

A strategy is a plan of action designed to achieve a particular goal. The word strategy has military connotations because it derives from the Greek word for army. However, 'strategy' is bandied about far too much without a full understanding of its meaning. True strategy is about acting, planning and executing like an army general. In a marketing sense, strategy is the thinking, planning and innovation, and challenging and sometimes frustrating work you do before executing plans. But the problem today is that brand and marketing managers are so busy taking care of business, they're not taking the time to think. Please take the time to sit, plan, think and ponder what your plan is for the future.

Most marketers I meet can't tell me the positioning statements of their top three, let alone top five, competitors. Test yourself right now: write down your three key competitors and the positioning statement that sits with their logo. Now go and check out their websites to see how accurate you were. This is homework you have to do before you enter the war room.

Even Microsoft's Bill Gates takes time out every six months. He hires a cabin in the country, completely disconnects from all technology so he can sit in peace and think about his business and the brand. Bill Gates, just like an army general, would never go to war unless he had done proper due diligence. He would know the plan of attack, have contingencies, know his enemy and have thought through all the possibilities. He would have all his resources lined up and ready to go—PR, website, brochures, sales team briefings, flyers, signage and so on—so that at a given time the implementation could commence.

The 80–20 principle states that 80 per cent of effects come from 20 per cent of causes. Applied to business, this principle means that 80 per cent of income comes from 20 per cent of customers (these should be your target audience). Eighty per cent of the success of your brand will come from 20 per cent of the things that you do. Getting your fundamentals right—that is, having the right perception targeted at the right people before you start spending money, time and energy on promotion, is the 20 per cent. The problem comes when people don't identify that 20 per cent and spend their time and money on all the wrong things.

I have had the pleasure of working with the British Olympic 400 metre hurdles medallist, Sally Gunnell, who puts it this way, 'Am I focused, and am I focused on the right things?' Most marketing and brand managers don't focus on the right things, if they are focused at all. Too many marketing managers confuse activity with accomplishment. Just because they're busy and juggling three or four things at once, they think that they are having a great impact on the brand. Are you focused and are you focused on the right things?

Go back to your marketing model and ensure that 80 per cent of your time is spent on the right 20 per cent. The important thing is to identify the key strategic issues and implement with precision. Don't try to do everything because no brand manager can cover everything. Act like a true general and you will reap the rewards.

Vibe status

➤ Are you effectively using PR to build your brand?

➤ Does your advertising have a demonstrated point of difference, an overt benefit and give your target a reason to believe?

➤ Do all the visuals you use to market your brand create a tone for it?

➤ Do the brands that you associate with elevate and improve the perception of your brand?

➤ Do you have contact with your target audience every 90 days?

➤ Have you removed the jargon from your company literature?

➤ Have you mapped out all of the potential contact points that sell your message to your target?

➤ Do you have a strategy? Are you focused and are you focused on the right things?

Chapter 5

Think differently

So far we've covered strategies for branding and how to go about creating the right perception in the mind of your target audience to give them a reason to buy from you and not your competitor. This chapter is all about you, the marketer. What about your future? How you can be the best you can be in your chosen field? What Australian brands need above all else are thinkers.

In his book *Zag* Marty Neumeier talks about how, historically, brands have spent considerable time and money investing in trademarks and patents for their ideas. There was incredible investment in product. In this day and age, however, this investment is now seen as irrelevant as brands leap-frog each other through innovation, making previous products redundant at an increasingly rapid rate. Thinking differently, and thus creativity, is the currency of the future. It's what separates you from everyone else. Once upon a time, brand differentiation used to be based around knowledge and who had that knowledge. But knowledge no longer holds that power. The next evolution was technology. If you had the latest technology you were thought to hold the power, but now if you purchase new technology, you know that it's only a matter of months before a newer, more powerful model will become available. So technology no longer holds that power either. The true power in any marketplace is in the creativity and thought processes that are behind these things.

Every company and its brand is at war and the winner of every battle is the brand with the most successful thinking, and, generally, that comes from you, the marketing person. Marketing, branding and communication are all a battle of the mind. Sun Tzu said, 'Every battle is won before it is fought'. Creativity and innovation are the key tools or weapons for any marketer or brand person and are only going to become a more valuable commodity in the future. You simply cannot rely on what you did yesterday to win the battle tomorrow. Bill Gates said, 'We are in an economic downturn but an innovation upturn'. The great leaders of the future will be the innovation leaders. People don't want to be sold to, they want to be helped. They don't have time for ads. They are searching for your authentic story and a reason to believe you.

They want you to do more than just be a brand. They're looking for generous brands. And the only way to satisfy all these needs is to think differently about every aspect of your brand.

Businesses used to consider advertising to be a major expense. Today innovation fills that role through the development of processes, teams and capabilities that enable you to challenge everything about your product, service and culture. Remove the ceilings and start to hold yourself to a world-class standard. As Dee Hock, the founder of Visa, said, 'The problem is never how to get new, innovative thoughts into your mind, but how to get old ones out'. It's the continuous effort of thinking differently, not strength or intelligence, that is the key to unlocking your brand's potential.

You must think differently and challenge everything.

The real power for you as a marketer, whether you are the CEO or managing director of an organisation, or a sole operator, comes from an individual thinking differently. This includes thinking differently about your media, your tone, your presentation, your generosity, your brand, your recruitment and your council. No longer can you do the same as everyone else. There is a big difference between marketing and brand managers, and thinkers and strategists. Anyone can implement the promotional part of the marketing model—that's just spending money. You must think differently and challenge everything. It's your thinking that gives your brand its vibe. Not the product, the advertising or the packaging, but your thinking. Why? Because your thinking is where it all starts. The vision, the strategy, the position, the winning and the losing. It's the strategic thinking behind the activity that creates a brand.

It is said that when Englishman Roger Bannister was attempting to be the first person to break the four-minute mile before Australian John Landy, he changed his thinking, and instead of focusing on trying to run a mile in four minutes, he decided to run four by 400 metres back to back, each one in 59 seconds. By thinking differently about how he could achieve this seemingly impossible goal, he became the first man to break the four-minute mile.

For any brand, marketing or communications person, creativity and innovation will be your greatest assets and they will be the currency of the future. What your customers want from you is different thinking. If you're not thinking differently, then why do they need you? So, what are you doing to foster your thinking?

Use a journal to record your ideas

How many great marketing or product ideas do you see in any given day? How many thought-provoking quotes, sayings or stories do you read or hear in any given week? I'm staggered by how few marketers use a journal to record these valuable bits of information. I've been 'journaling' for the last five to seven years and it's made an immeasurable difference to the quality and process of my thinking, as well as my ability to articulate and deliver my material. After all, that's what marketers do — we collect stories and tell them in an interesting way through our brand. My recommendation is to buy yourself a good journal and start collecting sayings, concepts, ideas, interesting names, promotional thoughts and advertising campaigns. You can even extend your journaling to record valuable thoughts or passages from your latest good read. Your journal can become one of your most valuable resources.

There have been many good books written on the power of journaling and I think it's an essential part of what any good marketer, brand manager or even CEO must do. Quite apart from the business advantages, journaling is quite simply good for the soul. By this, I don't mean keeping a diary of daily activities — it's the collecting of thoughts and ideas, and inspirational, motivational or potentially helpful tips and tools that you can use in your own world.

Make time to think differently

You can't swim forever. There are times when it's valuable to rest, reflect and take time out from the stream of information. Too many brand managers are working *in* the brand instead of *on* the brand. You need to take time to look not only outside your own category, but also give your own creative spirit a chance to work. Leonardo da Vinci said, 'There's no room in a busy mind for creativity'. Your customers are using you because you can solve their problem better than the next person. And if you can't, why do they need you? If their problems today are different from their problems tomorrow, it means that you must be consistently thinking differently.

Thinking differently must become an important part of your day. I guarantee that if you went to your diary right now, there would be no time specifically allocated to thinking. By this I mean time where you can disconnect from your BlackBerry, iPhone, iPod, laptop and the world in general, to sit and think differently about your brand. What's one great idea for your brand worth? It could be worth thousands or millions of dollars! One great idea executed well could keep a single client for the next five years.

Thinking differently must become an important part of your day.

Creativity is a learned skill. It's something you can get better at, but you have to invest the time and make it an important part of your world. If you don't, then it's simply not going to happen. It's often said that people are the greatest asset to an organisation, but I'm not so sure. I believe that it's actually people's *thinking* that is the greatest asset. The same marketing manager can be a star today and a liability tomorrow. Today you're working with a brand and doing great things and challenging the way things have been done before, but overnight you decide to leave and go somewhere else and suddenly for the next four weeks you've become a liability. It's important to separate the thinking from the role. It's not you the marketer, it's your thinking that is the asset. The more you develop your thinking, the greater asset you will be for your company and the more valuable you'll become to your clients, and hence the more rewards you will reap. The world needs more thinkers who can challenge the way things are today to be prepared for tomorrow. But remember, you need to actually do something with your thinking. Indeed, as US humorist Will Rogers said, 'Remember, even if you're on the right track, if you just sit there you'll get run over'. It's all very well to be a great thinker, but at the end of the day for something to happen, something has to move.

Be your own brand

As an aside, people often ask me how you can create and market yourself as a brand. Oprah, Donald Trump, Shane Warne, Kate Moss, Paris Hilton, Karl Lagerfeld, Elle Macpherson, Richard Branson, George Gregan and, yes, even Kevin Rudd, have all created a brand out of their name.

An example of a real case study is when I was asked to work with the CEO of a large bespoke merchant bank who had approached me to help him with his own personal brand. He said, 'I'm often pitching to joint venture partners to come on board for business propositions that we are putting together, and at the end of my presentation the other CEOs in the room will look directly at me and ask why I should be the one to run it. I need to be clear about what my position is so I can answer that question in a precise, confident and professional manner. That's why I need you to help me with my brand'.

So we got together and talked through the model: Who's the target? Tell me about them? What do you do, specifically? Most importantly I got him to talk about why he is different from other CEOs who could run the business—and it was here that the answer presented itself.

We'd been talking about where he'd come from, his successes, his failures, what he thought his strengths were and why he would be a good choice to run any joint venture that he brought partners in to be involved with. It was during this time that he said one simple phrase that summed it all up. I got up from the chair, wrote it on the whiteboard and he sat there in amazement and said, 'That's it'. It often happens like this, where the answer is not technical, but something you hear your target audience or your team say in conversations. The most powerful positionings are when they are in the language of the people you are talking to.

He sent me an email a couple of days later saying that in the past two days he had presented to two lots of joint venture partners. At the end of each presentation he asked, 'You're probably wondering why me? It's quite simple', at which point he would outline his own personal brand position and what it meant. He said knowing what his personal position was gave him power on the floor and made him feel good, and he was also able to proactively answer their question before they had time to ask it. This little statement has since become his motto. He's been able to use it in presentations and when doing business with his own teams. It sets the foundations for the standards and thinking he holds himself to.

For more information on taking the fundamentals at the beginning of this book and applying them personally — for example, if you work for a company and are in the process of working your way up the corporate ladder — check out my book *Who Stole My Mojo?*

Vibe status

➤ What are you doing to stimulate your mind to think differently about your brand?

➤ Are you recording your ideas and thoughts in a journal?

➤ Are you taking time out to think differently about your brand?

Chapter 6

Final thoughts

<small>otion category brands marketers service company product promotion position better create competitors marketing uct customers better s money positioning statement media tough times client awareness model perception fundamentals target networking successful mind need people manager Apple creating think marketing mod e different strategy communicate defining websites audience Woolwor business question time growth words base camp vibe different</small>

Now that we're almost at the end of the book, I encourage you to think about the journey we've been on — from the fundamentals of marketing and branding to the modern-day trends that are changing the face of branding and how these things help to generate a vibe for your brand.

Base camp

Sir Ranulph Fiennes, said to be the world's greatest living explorer, in his book *Mad, Bad and Dangerous to Know* told of his journey climbing Mount Everest and his battle with altitude sickness. If a climber ascends too quickly without acclimatising on the way up, he or she can get severely ill and the climb is essentially finished. This is also true for marketing and branding. If you move too quickly away from the fundamentals to take advantage of trends, then your brand is more likely to get altitude sickness. As you continue to bring more and more sophistication to your brand, you always need regularly to check back in with base camp.

Base camp is your marketing model. It is a series of core questions: Who's the target? What's the product? What's the category? What word do you want to own? What's your positioning statement? How have you told the story? No matter how sophisticated your brand, new media trends or even changes in the marketing team, you must always revisit base camp. Often once people get the fundamentals in place they get so carried away with the implementation that they forget about their positioning and core focus. Remember that when telling your story, marketing is not only a conversation, it's an evolution. To evolve the brand you must constantly go back and check in with base camp.

The world's highest profile investor Warren Buffett has said, 'When the tide goes out, you can see who's wearing bathing suits'. This is a great analogy for base camp. While business is good and everything is bubbling along nicely, people are happy with their marketing and their brand. However, it's during tough economic times that suddenly the tide goes out and you can see who really has a strong, resilient brand and those who have been fortunate to ride the crest of a wave. Now is the time to pull on a bathing suit because the tide is going out. Now more than ever you have to have a tight base camp.

Crunch time

Towards the end of 2008, when the world's financial system was under stress and there was considerable debate about how long the period of uncertainty would last, I was asked regularly about the best way to market a brand during challenging economic times. My answer was that as no-one had been through a period quite like this, there was no one correct answer. Of course, getting your fundamentals in place was still the most important part of any marketing model, but there was one important difference. Whereas previously the main decision of any consumer was what to buy and who to buy from, it became more a matter of whether anything needed to be done at all.

...you must constantly go back and check in with base camp.

If the answer is no, that nothing really needs to be done, then the customer's problem is solved. If the answer is yes, then the next question is, who will I buy from? That's when it comes down to the customer making a choice between you and your competitor. So in tough economic times, not only does your perception have to differentiate you from your competitors, it also has to motivate people to *do something* (rather than nothing). In uncertain times, consumers and businesses weigh up every problem, asking whether they need to spend money or whether they can get by without it. If they think they can get by without it, then they need to be convinced otherwise. If they decide to do something, then they need to be convinced to use your product or service.

This may sound fairly basic, but in challenging times remember to ensure you have your fundamentals in place, then aim to get the consumer motivated to do something. After that you can get to work on getting them to purchase your product rather than someone else's.

Never compete, never compare

One of my favourite quotes, and one that I think should be an anthem for any brand manager or company leader, is something that I heard fashion designer Karl Lagerfeld once say. Lagerfeld is the creative genius behind brands such as Chanel and Fendi, as well as his own brand, Karl Lagerfeld. When asked to judge a photographic exhibition by designer Tommy Hilfiger, he replied, 'I find this very hard; I've always lived by the motto never compete, never compare'. Never compete, never compare — what a fantastic motto!

My challenge to marketers today, no matter what category, industry, or business you work in, is to neither compete with nor compare yourself with other brands in your category. Yes, you should be aware strategically of what your competitors are doing and how they're doing it, but primarily when you're thinking of new and innovative ways to present yourself, you should aim to move into virgin territory. You need to think differently and set your own path. It has been said that if you are following the footsteps of others you'll never overtake them. The reason that people love many of the brands that I've mentioned in this book is because they've forged their own path. This does of course involve some risk, and not everything is going to work out necessarily as planned, but that's all part of the ride. I've spoken on a number of occasions with people who have worked with Steve Jobs at Apple. They have commented that he isn't afraid of, and in some cases he welcomes, failure, because if he's failing it means he's trying something different and something new.

Create your own vibe and be aware of, but not driven by, others. Don't endeavour to go forward by continually looking over your shoulder at everyone else.

You go to a party

Just in case I haven't made the distinction between marketing, advertising, public relations, design and branding clear up to this point, the following story may help resolve any uncertainty you have.

You go to a party, see a woman who takes your fancy, walk up to her and say, 'I'm a great lover'—that's marketing. You go to a party, see a woman, walk up to her and say, 'I'm a great lover, I'm a great lover, I'm a great lover'—that's advertising. You go to a party and you overhear two women talking about you, and one says to the other, 'Trust me, he's a great lover'—that's PR. You go to a party, walk up to a woman, say nothing but you think loving thoughts and look longingly into her eyes—that's graphic design. You go to a party, meet a woman, the next day you ring her, she says hello and you say, 'I'm a great lover'—that's telemarketing. You go to a party, a woman walks over to you and says, 'Hi, I understand you're a great lover'—that's when you become a brand!

... to succeed in marketing and branding, you have to love the game.

When somebody walks up to you and repeats back to you the perception you would like them to have of you, your company, brand or service, that's when you become a successful brand.

For the love of the brand

After finishing a speech at a seminar in Adelaide, a young guy from the audience approached me and asked whether I did any lecturing at university. I actually don't do any lecturing, but the question did make me think about what I would say to a younger audience. One of the most important things I would say is that to succeed in marketing and branding, you have to love the game. It's about loving the whole industry—marketing, branding, communication, PR, promotion, social networking, new media, the whole vibe. You need to become a student of the game and love it.

The best marketing strategists I know love the game. They're constantly sourcing new material. They look at magazines purely for the ads and are always searching for the next great angle that they can apply to their own brand. They spend time in supermarkets scouring the shelves researching who did what and why. They walk through the cosmetics section of department stores seeing what they can use or adapt to their own brand. A different industry gives them fodder for innovative ideas that they can bring to their own category.

The truly great marketing and brand strategists admire other people's work, they aspire to be the best they can be and they take great pride in, and see as a challenge, the opportunity to go to battle with a competitor. They know that sometimes they'll win, sometimes they'll lose, but they love the game either way. Although they have a healthy ego, they're not caught up in it and it doesn't inhibit them or stop them from learning, exploring or trying new things. I think there's a lot to be said for this. If you love the game and everything about it, you'll reap great rewards, and there is no greater reward than winning the space in the mind of your target audience where they actually fall in love with your brand.

Yeah, but what if?

At the end of every presentation I give I welcome questions from the audience. Often those questions take the form of, 'Yeah, what you've said is all very well, but what if...' I'm pretty sure you may have even had one or two thoughts of this nature while reading this book. Here are some of the most common 'Yeah, but what if' questions that I'm asked. I want to share them with you here because if one person is asking them, then I'm sure a larger number are thinking them.

Yeah, but what if I have only one or two clients?

It doesn't really matter if you have only one or two clients. If that client has the choice of either doing nothing or doing something, then you still have to market yourself. Although you may have only one or two clients right now, if it's a category worth chasing, there are more competitors coming. If you create a perception and own a word, then you reduce the options of any new entrants to the category to own. Also, creating a perception in the mind of those clients will be the springboard that keeps them comfortable moving forward with you. The easiest way for you to grow your revenue is to get more business from the customers or clients you currently have. The marketing model is as appropriate for you as it is to Coca-Cola, which is marketing to anyone with a mouth. As long as you have a core target with a problem that needs fixing, you need to give them a reason to choose you over someone else, as opposed to doing nothing. If you don't stand for something, you stand for nothing.

Yeah, but what if I'm in a service industry?

I appreciate that, at first glance, the principles discussed in this book appear to be more difficult to apply to a service industry, as you don't necessarily have a tangible product such as a Mars Bar, a can of dog food or piece of technology to market to your target audience. However, a service in itself can also be a product, and you still need to create a perception. Ask yourself: if I could do something or do nothing, then why should I do something? If there is a choice to be made between services, then why should I choose yours?

When I worked with members of the New Zealand insurance industry, they claimed that 40 per cent of their customers were currently underinsured. So their challenge was not only to sell to new customers, but also to create the perception among their current customers that they were underinsured and should consider upgrading their insurance level. If you still don't believe service industries need marketing, then think about who your superannuation is currently held with. Who is your car insurance with? Who does your tax? Who provides your legal services? Which doctor do you go to? All of these services have been selected by you because of a particular perception they have in the marketplace. If they haven't given you a compelling reason to use them, then they haven't marketed themselves as a brand.

If you don't stand for something, you stand for nothing.

Yeah, but what if I have no money?

'Yeah, but what if I have no money?' is probably one of the greatest ceilings I come across, and it's my belief that the minute we think we have no money we stop thinking about how we can communicate with our target audience. Once again, I maintain it's not a money thing, it's a thinking thing. Brands such as Molton Brown go about marketing themselves while spending little or no money. Starbucks has little advertising, yet it has managed to create a global brand. Don't let budgetary constraints create a ceiling over the standards to which you hold your brand. Having no money just means you need to think more creatively about your brand. More than likely you have a website. Have you thought about a blog? Which elephants are you dancing with? Networking is free. Building a perception through your current materials is free. Often it's doing what you're already doing, but just doing it properly. If you're in business, then you probably already have a business card, a letterhead, a website and an email address. These are four areas that you can work on to start building a strong perception in the mind of your target.

Yeah, but what if I'm in business-to-business?

I'm regularly asked, 'Yeah, but what if I'm in business-to-business?' Who printed your business cards and why? Who did you buy your laptop from and why? Who did you buy your mobile phone from and why? Who did you buy your stationery from and why? Whoever you bought your own business-to-business (B2B) things from, the reasons you bought from them was all due to perception. That's branding. Everyone who is in business has had to buy business equipment or outsource something to another supplier. This is the marketing that builds perception. B2B is no different, except instead of your target being a grocery buyer with two children, yours might be an organisation with 500 staff or more who have a mobile sales team who need telecommunications systems. B2B just means you have a different target and that you sell a product that suits the business industry. Don't let B2B be a ceiling over your thinking.

I'm sure there are more 'Yeah, but what ifs' that I haven't covered. I invite you to contact me if you have your own 'Yeah, but what if' questions because chances are, if you're thinking them, then others will be as well. Please send me your 'Yeah, but what ifs' either via my website <www.garybertwistle.com> or you can find me on Twitter (GaryBertwistle) and I will address your issues and share your concerns with the rest of the marketing, branding and communications community.

Don't let budgetary constraints create a ceiling over... your brand.

□ □ □

This book was written to stimulate your thinking. Not everything I've talked about will be appropriate for you. There will be things that I've mentioned that you don't agree with, and that's okay, provided it has at least stimulated your thinking. But if you have found one or two great nuggets that you can take away to make a difference to your marketing and assist you in creating an outstanding brand, then it's been a worthwhile investment of your time and money.

Well, that's it! I hope you've found *The Vibe* valuable and are feeling motivated and inspired. Let's finish as we began, with Dennis Denuto's quote from *The Castle*: 'It's the constitution, it's Mabo, it's justice, it's law, it's the vibe and ... no, that's it, it's the vibe'. The brand is all about the vibe. It's about the perception, it's about the customer and client. It's about your people, your media, being more than a brand and being generous. It's about not allowing ceilings to hold back your brand's growth and development. It's about your packaging, presentation, your publicity and your environment. It's about creativity, it's about base camp and it's about you the marketer. Your brand is the vibe.

Whether or not your brand becomes world-class is a matter for conjecture. Other people will be the judge of that. What you *can* control is whether you are prepared to take the necessary steps to create an outstanding vibe for your brand. If you have an outstanding vibe, people can't help but fall in love with your brand, and that's the most powerful position for any marketer to be in.

Further reading

Gary Bertwistle, *Who Stole My Mojo? How to Get It Back and Live, Work and Play Better*, Allen & Unwin, Crows Nest, New South Wales, 2008.

Donny Deutsch & Peter Knobler, *Often Wrong, Never in Doubt: Unleash the Business Rebel Within*, HarperCollins, New York, NY, 2005.

Seth Godin, *The Dip: A Little Book that Teaches You When to Quit (and When to Stick)*, Penguin Group (USA), New York, NY, 2007.

Seth Godin, *Meatball Sundae: Is Your Marketing out of Sync?*, Portfolio, New York, 2007.

Doug Hall, *Jump Start Your Business Brain: Scientific Ideas and Advice that Will Immediately Double Your Business Success Rate*, Eureka Institute, Cincinnati, Ohio, 2001.

Lois Kelly, *Beyond Buzz: The Next Generation of Word-of-Mouth Marketing*, AMACOM, New York, NY, 2007.

Noah Kerner & Gene Pressman, *Chasing Cool: Standing Out in Today's Cluttered Marketplace*, Atria Books, New York, NY, 2007.

Marty Neumeier, *Zag: The Number One Strategy of High-Performance Brands*, New Riders, Berkeley, California, 2007.

Al Ries & Jack Trout, *Positioning: The Battle for Your Mind*, McGraw-Hill, New York, NY, 2001.

Al Ries & Jack Trout, *The 22 Immutable Laws of Marketing*, Profile Books, 1994.

Carl Sewell, *Customers for Life: How to Turn that One-Time Buyer into a Lifetime Customer*, Currency Books, New York, NY, 2002.

Sun Tzu, *The Art of War*, trans. Samuel B Griffith, Oxford University Press, London, 1971.

Sam Walton, *Sam Walton: Made in America*, Bantam, New York, NY, 1993.

Index

Gary

BERTWIST/E

Unlock your great ideas

Visit <www.garybertwistle.com> for information about having Gary unlock your great ideas with a keynote speech to you and your team, as well as free podcasts, vidcasts and book reviews. You can also subscribe to *The Espresso* (the world's first newspaper for thinkers) and have it delivered free to your desktop every week!

ON THE ROAD TO FINDING A CURE

Cancer is one of the world's greatest takers of life. Cancer does not discriminate. It affects men, women and children alike and it must be stopped.

In a coffee shop in Sydney in 2007 Gary sat with a friend of his, Geoff Coombes, and had the idea for a charity event. An endurance athlete, Gary wanted to do something that was long. A cyclist, Geoff wanted to do something on the bike. Together they formed the Tour de Cure. What started as a dream in a coffee shop, within six months became a reality when a team of 26 cyclists and five support crew set out from Brisbane and rode to Sydney for the inaugural Tour de Cure. Since then the tour has ridden from Melbourne to Sydney and in 2009 Brisbane to Cairns.

As one of the co-founders of this charity, the Tour de Cure has become a big part of Gary's life. So many people are affected in some way by cancer, and Gary is committed to making a difference by raising funds not only to provide treatment options for sufferers and support for families, but ultimately to find a cure. Visit <www.tourdecure.com.au>.